PRIMARY SOURCES IN AMERICAN HISTORY

CONSULTING EDITOR   Grady McWhiney

IMPERIALISTS VERSUS ANTI-IMPERIALISTS:
The Debate Over Expansionism in the 1890's
Edited by **Richard E. Welch, Jr.**

SLAVERY IN AMERICA: Theodore Weld's
American Slavery As It Is
Edited by **Richard O. Curry** and **Joanna Dunlap Cowden**

OVER THERE: EUROPEAN REACTION TO
AMERICANS IN WORLD WAR I
Edited by **Robert C. Walton**

AMERICAN UTOPIANISM

ROBERT S. FOGARTY

ANTIOCH COLLEGE

F. E. PEACOCK PUBLISHERS, INC.

ITASCA, ILLINOIS 60143

JOHN W. CAUGHEY, Advisory Editor

Foreword

It is not easy to understand the past. A good textbook helps by providing what its author—usually a distinguished historian—considers the essential facts and his interpretation of those facts. A good instructor also helps. But the student, if he is to be other than a parrot, must be exposed to more than one or two viewpoints. Told that authorities disagree, the student is likely to ask: "But which interpretation is *right*?"

At that point he is ready to do some research himself—to read and to evaluate what certain persons who actually saw an event wrote about it. Sampling original sources on which historical interpretations are based is not only an exciting experience; it adds flavor to knowledge. Furthermore, it encourages the student to weigh conflicting evidence himself and to understand historical variety and complexity.

The Primary Sources in American History series provides the documents necessary to explore the past through the eyes of those who lived it. Edited and introduced by an able scholar, each volume in the series contains contemporary material on some historical topic or period—either a collection of varied sources (letters, diaries, memoirs, reports, etc.), or a new edition of a classic eyewitness account.

Grady McWhiney
Editor

Table of Contents

Introduction

Any visitor to California these days hears a good deal about communes and their bearded inhabitants who are (depending on your informant) Communists, lovers of the earth, or dropouts. That they might be all three seems too complex to the casual sightseer. To any student of American communitarianism, however, the present California scene is an old one — so old that it predates the Revolution (1776) and may have arrived in the *Susan Constant*.

The tradition itself is as old as Plockhoy's Commonwealth (1663) on the banks of the Delaware which grew out of a 1659 document: *A Way Propounded to Make the Poor in These and Other Nations Happy, by Bringing Together a Fit, Suitable and Well Qualified People unto One Household-Government, or Little-Common-Wealth.* Plockhoy's Mennonite colony lasted only a year, as the English conquest of New Netherlands resulted in the plunder of "what belonged to the Quaking Society of Plockhoy to a very naile." Since that first communitarian effort there have been over 500, including the present psychedelic activity. The conditions of American life — particularly in the pre-Civil War period — were conducive to utopian efforts. The belief that men could remake their institutions by "reasoned choice" has been central to American ideology. Our most astute writer on communitarianism, Arthur Bestor, has pointed out that the American community builders rejected individualistic, revolutionary, and reformist alternatives for "patent-office models"

of the good society. In short, the experimenters were model
builders paving the way to the future by example and peaceful exhortation.

The period between 1820 and 1860 saw the proliferation of
communities, as religious and sectarian efforts blossomed under the spirit of millenial and revival fervor and the influence
of the philosophies of Robert Owen and Charles Fourier.
With the decline of revivalism and the steady emergence of
an industrial empire, the arcadian models lost favor, and, in
fact, relevance. Some of the religious communities, like Oneida and Amana, persevered in the post-Civil War period, but
their biblical vision did not excite very many similar efforts.
The publication of Bellamy's *Looking Backward* (1888) and
the rise of labor and socialist groups signaled the emergence
of a new tradition. Whereas New York and Ohio had been
the centers of earlier utopian activity, California now led.

The range of communitarian activity throughout the 19th
century was extraordinary: It included free lovers, celibates,
anarchists, socialists and spiritualists. There was always a
strong spiritualist tradition — notably among the Shakers — but
it remained essentially submerged until the late 19th century
and the ascendancy of theosophical societies. Twentieth century experiments were much more modest — both in numbers
and aspirations — since both religious millenialism and socialist hopes declined.

The period since World War I has been characterized by
antiurban and subsistence farming themes — much of it conservative in tone and emphasis. Social planners and in-
novators were found increasingly within the framework of
society as the federal government encouraged and occasionally subsidized such individuals. Whereas Robert Owen had
taken out ads in the London newspapers, Ralph Borsodi was
employed by the Department of Agriculture. A reaction
against the planned society — complemented by a drug-
centered and politicized youth culture — produced the current

crop of utopians—with organic gardening rather than a Graham table, converted vans rather than wagons, and the *I Ching* rather than Owen's *A New View of Society*.

The purpose of this collection is to let the reader see the world through communitarian eyes, in the words of the participants or firsthand observers.

Ephrata

The German pietist community of Ephrata was the first significant communitarian effort in America in terms of longevity and influence. Founded by Conrad Beissel in 1732 (some 12 years after his arrival from Eberbach, Germany), the community was celibate, ascetic, and pacifist.

Beissel's *Mystical Sentences* (the first book of German poetry published in America) reflects this strain, and his hymns exerted a strong influence on early American music. The community excelled in the printing of books and the construction of illuminated manuscripts.

Beissel died in 1768 and was succeeded by Peter Miller (Prior Jabez) who had come to America in 1730 as a minister of the Reformed Church but was swept up in an 1735 revival which led him to Ephrata. Miller was a classical scholar and a member of the American Philosophical Society, but such gifts could not arrest the society's decline after Beissel's death.

1. Ninety-Nine Mystical Sentences

Peter Miller translated part of Beissel's 1730 "sentences" and sent a copy to his fellow Philosophical Society member and the original publisher of the "Nine and Ninety Mystical Proverbs" — Benjamin Franklin.

"A Unique Manuscript by Peter Miller" edited by Julius F. Sachse (Pennsylvania-German Society, 1912), pp. 11–33.

NINETY NINE MYSTICAL SENTENCES, PUBLISHED FOR THE SCHOLLARS OF DIVINE WISDOM BY THE REV: FATHER CONRAD BEISSEL AND PRINTED AT PHILADA. BY B. FRANKLIN

Anno 1730

1. To know truly himself, is the highest Perfection; and to worship and adore right the only, everlasting and invisible God in Jesus Christ, is Life eternal.

2. All wickedness is Sin: yet is none so great, but to be separated from God.

3. Whosoever loveth God, is from God, and hath the unigenite Son remaining in himself, for the same did proceed from God.

4. The highest Wisdom, is, to have no Wisdom: yet is he the highest, which possesseth God, for He is alone Wise.

5. All Works, which a man Worketh, bring him to that End, for which they are calculated, either for God's or his own Self's sake.

6. Build no Temple without Jerusalem, lest thou mightest offer thy Gifts to a Foreigner, and he also might reward thee.

7. Carry no Fire in a Wooden Vessel, lest it might burn thee but build an Alter from new Stones, and put thereon good Frankincence, and let the Fire of divine Love penetrate the same: then shall a pleasant Odour raise before his holy Nose.

8. Be always little and humble in a high Station, and raise not they Building high, before thou has measured the Depth, lest thou mightest in thy ascending come above the Measure, and thy Building be destroyed.

9. And build not for thyself a Seat in Heaven, before thou hast made the Earth thy Footstool: lest thou mightest have chosen the Earth for the Heaven.

10. Fight with nothing, which proves to mighty for thee: yet keep good watch with thyself, lest thou mightest be killed by thine own Domestiks.

11. Build thine House with Industry, and make its Foundation in the Depth, and let it be supported by Pillars: and when thou commest to the Roof thereof, study to make a good Covering, whereunder thou mayst hide thyself in Cloudy Seasons, and mightest not perish in Time of Distress.

12. Beware thine Heart against Night-Thieves, yet take good care,

lest the Noon-Devil with his Angels might enter into thy Garden, and bite off the Eyes of thine Vines: which is worse, than when the wild Boars break in, for those only rout the Soil.

. . . . .

94. Neither be a Glutton or luxurious, lest thou mayst ruin thy Estate by debauching in Prosperity: and then suffer Want in Need.

95. Distribute thine Bread among the Hungry, and if thou dost see any nacked, cloth him: then thou shalt gather a Treasure in Distress and Provision for many Years.

96. Be not wise with thyself, before thou hast travelled through the way of Folly: lest thou mayst possess Folly for Wisdom.

97. And put no Trust in thyself, until thou are confounded in thy best Works: for none is good, except the only God.

98. Ascend not too high, before thou hast measured the Depth: lest in thy Ascending thou mayst come too high, and another might cast thee down.

99. To be little and low in his own Eyes, is the Victory in the Power of God.

2. Visit of Israel Acrelius

Israel Acrelius, a Swedish minister, visited Ephrata in 1753 when both Beissel and Miller were involved actively with the community.

Ephrata is a place in Lancaster county, Pennsylvania, eleven and a half English miles from the town of Lancaster, in Cocalicoa township, situate on the Cocalicoa creek, between two hills. It is a Protestant cloister, having in possession about one hundred and thirty acres of land, well situated, and built with a number of wooden houses at some distance apart, with apple-trees planted in the intervening spaces. There are also grape-vines there of a good quality, but not in any great number.

Israel Acrelius, *A History of New Sweden,* translated by William Reynolds (Philadelphia, 1874), pp. 373–99.

The people who live here are called by the English, Dumplers, by the Germans, Dunkers, from *"duncken"* or *"tuncken,"* "to dip," as they are a kind of Anabaptists. From this the town is called by a nickname, but generally *Dunkers' Town.*

The arrangement of the cloister-life was made by Conrad Beisel, formerly a German burgher, who still lives in Ephrata, or Dunkers' Town, as the Director of the whole community, and he is now about 64 years of age. He is a small, lean man, has gray and bushy hair, is quick in his utterance as well as in his movements. Twenty-two years since he first chose for himself the life of a hermit, building for this purpose a small house on the banks of the Cocalicoa. After some time he took a notion to establish a society of his own, upon principles derived in part from other sects, and in part the product of his own brain. His undertaking prospered, and Germans of both sexes came thither, united with him, and made him their priest, chief man, and director of the whole society, not only of the cloister, but of all the brethren in their faith living in this country. From this time he called himself *"Friedsam"* (Peaceful); as it is also an established regulation in their society, that all who are admitted among them shall receive a new name in baptism, as a sign that they have come into a new condition, different from that of the great and wicked world. The brethren and sisters call him Father Friedsam, which is also his common name in the country. He calls himself *"Friedsam, the elder brother."* He preaches among them, and administers the sacraments as a Minister. As a Director, he makes laws and regulations.

Next to him is a chief over the cloister, or, as they call it, the *"Community."* His name is Eleazar; suggested, undoubtedly, by the office which he exercises in the economy of the cloister, that is, to receive and distribute the provisions, to purchase clothing according to the wants of the convent, also food and the like. He was now 42 years old, and had lived nineteen years in the fraternity. His father, 60 years of age, was also in the convent, but, as he had come in later, his son was his superior. A similar arrangement also exists among the Nuns.

There was also a brother named Jabez, who, before his rebaptism, was called Peter Miller. He had been a German Calvinistic Minister, came into the country, according to their custom, as a candidate for the Ministry in the Reformed Church of the country, was afterwards ordained by the Presbyterian Minister, Mr. Andrew, in Philadelphia, and for a long time preached in various parts of the country among the Germans before that, eighteen years since, he betook himself to Ephrata. He is a learned man, understands the Oriental languages, speaks Latin, discusses theological controversies as well as other sciences; although, in his present condition, he has forgotten much. He is of a good stature, with a friendly face and friendly manners, on which account strangers always get introduced to him, and seek his society. He is open-hearted towards those to whom he takes a liking, and is modest and genial. The brethren have great respect for him, and not without reason, for he is a prudent man, upon whom their order chiefly depends, although he gives himself no higher name than that of a simple brother. In their Public Worship he reads the Scriptures, and also baptizes when so directed by Father Friedsam.

Father Friedsam lives by himself in a little house between the brothers' and the sisters' cloisters, being waited upon by the brethren, and has his food from their kitchen. He lives in entire solitude, except when messengers go out or in, or he performs his duties in the congregation.

The brethren have their convent below, for the houses stand near to each other, with their rear running back to the stream. It is three stories high, and contains about one hundred rooms. The cells are about four paces long and two broad, and there are usually three cells to each antechamber. There is one man to each cell. One iron stove usually serves to warm two or three rooms. The house has a wing. In the lowest story is the brethren's church, in the next their refectory, in the uppermost their store-rooms for their economical purposes. All their doors are unusually narrow, the stairs steep and narrow, so that other people find difficulty in getting along them. The windows are in like manner small. No chair is seen in their rooms, but only narrow benches; but these as well as the floor are just as clean and bright as though they had been newly scoured. The inside of the house is plastered and whitewashed.

The sisters' convent, standing by itself, is built on the hill above, and arranged in a similar manner, having its own refectory and its own church in a wing of the house. They have also some other small houses for work close by.

The business of the brethren outside of the house is to work in the fields, meadows, and woods, as also at their mill. The greater part of them seemed to be brought up to agricultural labors. Others labor inside of the convent at all sorts of handicrafts, such as shoemaking, tailoring, weaving cloth and stockings, and the like, partly for the use of the cloisters and partly for sale, and so as to enable them to purchase other necessaries. Others attend to other domestic duties, such as cooking, baking, house-cleaning, washing clothes, etc., for all the work is done by the brethren without any female assistance in the men's cloister.

The sisters also live by themselves in their convent, engaged in spinning, sewing, writing, drawing, singing, and other things. The younger sisters are mostly employed in drawing. A part of them are just now constantly engaged in copying musical note-books for themselves and the brethren. I saw some of these upon which a wonderful amount of labor had been expended.

The dress of the brethren is a long, close coat, the skirts of which overlap each other, and are fastened with hooks quite down to the feet, with narrow sleeves, and the collar fitted close around the neck; also a girdle around the middle of the coat. When they wish to be well dressed, a habit is also worn over the close coat, like a chasuble in front, which is thrown over the head; but back of the head is a cape or hood to draw over the head in bad weather, and below this a round cape which hangs down over the back. In summer-time the clothes are of linen or cotton, and entirely white; in the winter-time they are of white woollen cloth. On work-days they have coarse coats usually fastened around them by a leathern girdle. But upon their Sunday-clothes the girdles are either of embroidered woollen stuff or linen. Members of the congregation living in the country dress like those in the cloisters when they come to their church. However, they have clothes of various colors and of the usual fashion. Some have inserted in front on their hoods a piece of pasteboard, which serves as a guard to the capoch when it is drawn over the head. The brethren of the convent wear no shirts, but have their woollen coats next to their body. In summer-time they go barefooted; if they wear shoes, they are either of the usual sort with strings, or they are of wool above and a leather sole below. Some wear straw hats when they are travelling over the country; but most of them use their cape or hood as a hat or cap.

The sisters' dress was also a long, close coat, but we noticed that they all had linen girdles. The hood which they always had over their heads was sewed on to the coat. Their coats are also of linen or cotton stuff in summer; in winter of wool, without any linen next to their body. They also go barefooted in summer.

This dress makes them look quite thin, which their scanty food aids.... Hence they are very quick and rapid in their movements, are not troubled by their narrow doors or their steep and narrow stairs. It seemed strange that they could go so thinly clad in the autumn.

.   .   .   .   .

They have a great many Jewish customs. They all have their beard growing up to their ears. This, together with their white dress and their spare diet, is well adapted to gain their object, namely, to look pale, thin, and wretched. They go barefooted in summer, use feet-washing, keep the seventh day as holy, count their hours after the Jewish fashion, from the beginning of the day, so that our six o'clock is their one, and our twelve their seven. To which may also be added that when I heard them read the Scriptures five different times, it was always out of the Old Testament, the Prophets, and the Psalms, but never out of the New Testament. So, also, they had a taste for the Old Testament in their "Sanctuary," and their "Women's gallery."

They hold with the Quakers, inasmuch as they are a sort of Enthusiasts. They do, indeed, read the Scriptures, but believe themselves to be possessed of an "inward light," which transcends the outward. They, therefore, despise all outward instruction; give out that their sermons come from the immediate light and impulse of the Spirit in the same time in which they speak; that each and every one has liberty to teach publicly in their congregations, when the order therefor comes; that we are to use "thou" in conversation; to shake hands; exhibit absolute perfection in our life, and to use no prayers, unless they come extempore into the head.

They agree with the Anabaptists in that they take no one into their Society unless he has been baptized by them; baptize those who come from other churches; baptize only those who have come to years of discretion. Their baptism is performed with an abundance of water by immersion; other things, as already mentioned. They also hold services in their churches late at night. Father Friedsam, who lives in a little house between the brethren's and sisters' cloisters, has a rope, which goes upon both sides over the garden, with a bell at each end in both cloisters. When it so comes into his head, and he pulls thereon, and the bell rings, and even if it were in the middle of the night, all must get up and assemble in their church to hold service; a small paper lantern in each one's cell is used upon such occasions.

With the Papists, also, they have much in common, although they call themselves Protestants; they follow the same cloistered life, and have a cloister dress, and also rules for their meals; they seek their justification by a severe life, and perfection in a life of celibacy; they believe in a purgatory, or purifying fire after death; on which account, also, Father Friedsam at certain times offers prayers for the dead. Many Roman Catholics from Germany have been received into their Society, and live among them. The number of people in the cloisters was much greater in former years. Now the brethren are not more in number than twenty-five (25), and the sisters thirty-five (35) or thirty-six (36). However earnestly they strive for a chaste life, the untimely intercourse of some of the brethren and sisters with each other has subjected the whole society to the unfavorable judgment of many. Father Friedsam himself is not free from such charges, which are made with great particularity. They cannot deny that some members have been licentious, but say that they have been immediately discarded; during the time that Conrad Weiser lived among them, he once took the liberty of visiting his own house and family in another place. But upon his return, after a strict examination, he had to submit to a severe punishment for having slept with his own wife, which he willingly underwent. Around the Convent and its land, families belonging to their Society have settled themselves and bought farms and homesteads. In this there is a policy, namely, that people of other faith may not come too near and disturb them. They are also so peaceful with their neighbors, that if any dispute ever arises, they would rather surrender their rights, or give the matter into the hands of others in whom they have confidence, than trouble any Judge with it. Their congregations are widely scattered in several places in Chester county, and also in East Jersey. But at some distance from the Convent several Hermits live in houses by themselves, built mostly at the expense of the Society.

They have one Society in New Virginia, upon New river. There, however, they dwell in separate houses, but in one neighborhood, and so by themselves that they neither help nor desire help from other people. The land that they cultivate has an excellent soil. The brethren often receive messages in these nests from travelling brethren, who always journey on foot, two and two together, never more and never less. Sometimes, also, the sisters are thus seen upon the roads.

Shakers

There can be little doubt that the Shakers were the most significant and enduring of the communities. The United Society of Believers in Christ's Second Coming had their origins in Bolton and Manchester, England, about 1747.

Ann Lee, the daughter of a Manchester blacksmith, was attracted to a group of "Shaking Quakers" in 1758 and assumed a position of leadership in 1772 after her imprisonment for disturbing the Sabbath and preaching a doctrine of celibacy. She believed sexual intercourse to be the root of all sin and saw the death of her four children in infancy as God's punishment. In 1774 she left England with nine others and settled eventually at Niskeyuna, New York. Under the influence of an intense revival passion, a group of New Light Baptists came upon Ann Lee's group in 1780. According to Edward D. Andrews:

There they found a fellowship literally following the example of the primitive apostolic church: men and women living together in celibate purity, holding all goods in common, working industriously with their hands, speaking and singing in unknown tongues, worshipping joyfully, preaching that Christ had come to lead believers to a perfect sinless, everlasting life — the life of the spirit.[1]

After her death in 1784 the Shakers were led by a remarkable series of leaders — most notably Joseph Meachem and

---

[1]Edward Deming Andrews, *The People Called Shakers* (New York: Dover Publications, Inc., 1963).

Frederick Evans. Meachem organized the society into "families" that were economically self-sufficient but looked toward the "central" family at New Lebanon, New York, for guidance and instruction. Evans had been active in the "Young America" movement and the Workingmen's Party prior to his conversion and was both well known and respected by American reformers.

At the time of the Civil War there were some 6,000 members in assorted communes from Hancock, Massachusetts, to Pleasant Hill, Kentucky. In 1891 the society still contained 1,700 members, but at present it has only a few adherents.

3. The Original Shakers in New England

William Plumer visited the Shaker communities at Harvard, Massachusetts, and Enfield, New Hampshire, in 1782 when he was 23. He later went on to become governor, senator, and chief justice from his state, but his early observations were that of a young man looking at a young society. The excesses that he notes were not representative of later Shaker groups, as prosperity brought on increased reserve.

(June 17, 1782.) Last week I paid the Shakers a visit at Harvard. I was received with civility and treated with kindness. I did not contradict them, but candidly and moderately inquired of them their origin and progress, their tenets and practice. This information was from their Elders and principal members. They say that in the year 1774 two women and three or four men, living at Manchester, in England, by an immediate and supernatural vision were directed to come to this country. They arrived at New York, but took up their residence in a country town (Watervliet), not far distant from Albany. One of these women, Anne Lee . . ., is the famous matron known as "The Elect Lady." She is generally attended by a number of her Elders. The select company that attends her are emphatically called "The Church." She frequently removes from town to town,

"The Original Shaker Communities in New England," *The New England Magazine*, 1900, pp. 304–6.

and constantly sends forth "laborers" as she calls them, to preach and teach her religion to the world. In some towns mobs have abused and insulted them; this they call persecution, and a proof of their being the true followers of that religion which is not of this world.

Their love and tenderness for each other degenerate into fondness and ridiculous weakness. They are very kind and attentive to strangers, so long as they have any prospect of converting them to their faith; but as soon as a man contradicts, or asks questions hard to answer, they become sullen, — pronounce him "damned," and avoid his company. Like the ancient Church, they consist principally of the lower class of people; few wise or learned men belong to their sect. They were formerly of different sects, but chiefly of those called "New Lights"; many of them were Baptists. They appeared very sober, serious, grave and solemn; honest and sincere in their profession; and in general much acquainted with the Scriptures. Before and after their eating, going to and returning from their beds, each of them falls on his knees, shaking, trembling, groaning, praying and praising. They affirm that they have the spirit of discerning and gift of prophecy, and have in fact predicted many things, with their contingent circumstances, long before these happened. Their dress is simple, plain and unadorned. The men have their hair short, and the women and children all wear strapped close caps.

They say that Christ promised to give his Church in all ages the power of working miracles; and that in fact they have healed the sick, cured cripples, and restored speech to the dumb. These mighty works were instantaneously effected by their praying and anointing the diseased with oil in the name of the Lord, — the patients having faith in God. On my expressing a desire to be present on such occasion, one of their Elders very sternly replied,"An evil and adulterous generation seeketh after a sign; but no sign shall be given unto *you*."

They generally assemble every evening, and frequently continue their exercises till after midnight. I went with them one evening to their meeting, and though they had cautioned me against being surprised at their worship, yet their conduct was so wild and extravagant that it was some time before I could believe my own senses. About thirty of them assembled in a large room in a private house, — the women in one end and the men in the other, — for dancing. Some were past sixty years old. Some had their eyes steadily fixed upward, continually reaching out and drawing in their arms and lifting up first one foot, then the other, about four inches from the floor. Near the centre of the room stood two young women, one of them very handsome, who whirled round and round for the space of fifteen minutes, nearly as fast as the rim of a spinning-wheel in quick motion. The violent whirl produced so much wind as kept her clothes as round and straight as though fastened to a hoop. As soon as she left whirling she entered the dance, and danced grace-fully. Sometimes one would pronounce with a loud voice, "Ho, ho," or "Love, love," — and then the whole assembly vehemently clapped hands for a minute or two. At other times some were shaking and trembling, others singing words out of the Psalms in whining, canting tones (but not in rhyme), while others were speak-ing in what they called "the unknown tongue," — to me an unintelli-gible jargon, mere gibberish and perfect nonsense. At other times the whole assembly would shout as with one voice, with one accord. This exercise continued about an hour; then they all retired to the sides of the room for a few minutes. Then the young lady who was the principal whirler walked into the middle of the room and began to dance. All the men and women soon joined her, — dancing, sing-ing, whirling, shouting, clapping their hands, shaking and trembling, as at first. This continued near an hour.

After a second intermission, two of the Elders, one after the other, addressed the audience; one of them delivering a very ingenious discourse in deference of their tenets and worship, with an ex-hortation to persevere in the ways of the Lord. He was a man of strong, clear, distinguishing mind, and an easy, yet impressive speak-er. More than half his discourse was in the strong, persuasive lan-guage of Scripture, well adapted to his purpose. Then the assembly renewed their former exercises for more than an hour. This done, several of the young people, both men and women, began to shake and tremble in a most terrible manner. The first I perceived was their heads moving from one shoulder to the other, — the longer they moved the quicker and more violently they shook. The motion proceeded from the head to the hands, arms and whole body, with such power as if limb would rend from limb. The house trembled as

if there were an earthquake. After this several young women embraced and saluted each other; two men embraced and saluted each
other; a third clasped his arms around both, a fourth around them,
and so on, until a dozen men were in that position, embracing and
saluting. I did not observe any man salute or embrace a woman, or
any woman a man; but as I was going to the meeting I had observed
a man and woman meet, when the woman with much eagerness
clasped and kissed the man's hand and arm and used the language of
a fond lover.

After meeting was done, I was invited by the Elders to take
lodging at their house, which I did. After a good supper they entered
into a long scriptural defence of their tenets and practices, resting
their religion solely on the authority of Scripture and testimony of
the Spirit. They admitted they could not support it by the reason and
nature of things. This conversation ended, the young woman who
had whirled the most began to shake and tremble astonishingly. She
told me this was not a voluntary motion, but that she was acted upon
by a supernatural impulse. I asked whether a man could, by his
strength, prevent her shaking and whirling. She said it would be
blasphemy against God to attempt such a thing. Some time after this,
when she was whirling with great velocity, I rose and advanced
gradually towards her, clasped her in my arms, and in the course of a
moment held her still, though she exclaimed against me as very rude
and indecent.

4. Millenial Laws

The Millenial Laws are a compendium of statutes that evolved
throughout the 19th century and were not formalized until 1845.
They represent the thoughts of Ann Lee as interpreted by Joseph
Meachem and Lucy Wright and modified by community practice
over the years.

Edward Deming Andrews, *The People Called Shakers* (New York: Dover
Publications, Inc., 1963), p. 253 ff.

PART I
THE GENERAL ORGANIZATION OF SOCIETY

The Order and Calling of Those in Lots of Care,
with the Duties of Members Thereunto

SECTION I
THE GENERAL ORGANIZATION OF SOCIETY

In societies of Believers which are sufficiently large to admit of it, the order of God requires a regular organization of families in order to accommodate and provide for the different circumstances of individuals in temporal things, and also for the advancement of spiritual travel in the work of règeneration, and the universal good of all the members, composing such society.

2. The orders, rules and regulations in each family, concerning things spiritual and temporal, should be such as are adapted to the protection, benefit and increase, of the numbers gathered therein.

3. The families should be of different classes, or grades, as to order, government and arrangement in things spiritual and temporal, adapted to the different situations and circumstances of members in society, and should be denominated — 1st or center family, generally called the Church of the society, — 2nd. Family. 3rd., 4th, etc. — or the name of each, may be such as is adapted to local circumstances, but their respective places in point of order, should be gradual and progressive.

4. The different orders and families, should in no wise have uncontrolled access to each other, by their communications either verbal or written, but all written communications and visits with each other, should be by the liberty of the Elders therein; and without such liberty, members should never go from one, to the other of said families.

5. The Church or center family, and as far as is practicable, each family that is gathered into order, should have a lot of Elders & Eldresses and a lot of Deacons and Deaconesses or Trustees, each lot of which should contain four or more persons, two of each sex.

6. The Church or center family, should be composed of such members, as are free from any involvements with those without, and such as are prepared by a previous privilege in families that are back, (where those who come in, over the age of thirteen, should be

first proved), to advance into a further degree of gospel order, in a
forward family, and a closer spiritual work of purification, and it
would be well, if all could come in at the gathering order, and be
measurably proved, before they advance further.

7. None should be gathered into the Church or first family, who
cleave unto their natural kindred of Fathers, Mothers, brothers,
sisters, husbands, or wives, houses or land; none should be gathered
into this order, but such as may by obedience stand spotless before
the Lord.

8. There should be a presiding Ministry in each society who
should have the general superintendence of all things of importance
therein, both spiritual and temporal, and to whom the Elders and
Trustees, (and through them the body of the people therein,) are
accountable for all their transactions. But two or more societies may
compose one Bishopric, as circumstances render it most proper.

9. Circumstances sometimes render it difficult to establish four
persons in lots of Elders and Deacons, of course no obligation to fill
the number, will apply in such cases, but four is considered the true
number, and it should never be neglected, unless driven thereto by
necessity.

SECTION II
THE ORDER OFFICE AND CALLING OF THE MINISTRY

The Holy Anointed at Holy Mount, (or New Lebanon,) are called
and chosen to stand as the first and leading Ministry, in the Zion of
God upon earth; unto whom all other orders of the Ministry, in all
other societies of Believers are accountable for all their transactions
of an official nature.

2. It is the right and duty of the Ministry if found necessary, to
alter or repeal certain orders, rules and regulations that may have
been established, or that may be established in the vineyard of
Christ and Mother upon earth. It is also their right to establish new
orders and regulations as far as they find it necessary.

3. It is the right and duty of the Ministry, in each society of
Believers, to establish such rules and regulations for the society over
which they preside as circumstances render necessary for the protection and benefit of the members thereof.

4. It is the right and duty of the Ministry to hold the Keys of the

Heavenly Kingdom of God upon earth, and to let nothing pass the doors of the House of God, or enter the gates of the Holy Vineyard below, that will in any wise, undermine the holy foundation on which it is built.

5. It is the privilege and duty of the Ministry at Holy Mount, (or center society,) to keep open the door of communication with other societies, in as much as it is their duty to link the golden chain of love and union, strength and blessing, throughout the Heavenly Vineyard of God, on earth, by such means as they in their wisdom see fit; — Therefore all visiting from place to place, must be done by their direction.

6. It is the privilege of the Ministry, to give to, or receive from other Believers, such gifts and presents, either spiritual or temporal, as they think will be a strength and benefit to them.

7. The Ministry may in no wise blend in common with the rest of the people; they may not work under the same roof, live in the same house, nor eat at the same table. But their dwelling place shall be in the meeting house, even in the most holy Sanctuary.

8. It is the right and duty of the Ministry in the center society, to go to other societies of Believers, in the land, as often as circumstances shall render it necessary, and they, in their wisdom, may deem it proper; for in their hands are placed the keys of the Holy and Heavenly Kingdom of God on earth.

9. And it is also the right of the Ministry in each Bishopric, in union with the Ministry at the center society, to make such visits there, as they find necessary from time to time, in order to keep unbroken the heavenly bond of union by which the Church of God is united in one.

·   ·   ·   ·   ·

SECTION II
ORDERS CONCERNING THE SPIRITUAL WORSHIP OF GOD, ATTENDING TO MEETINGS &C.

Believers are required by the orders of God, to retire to their rooms in silence, for the space of half an hour, and labor for a sense of the gospel, before attending meeting.

2. All should sit erect in straight ranks in retiring time, or if infirmity render it necessary, they may stand erect or walk the floor

in the fear of God, and attend to the reading of the hymn or anthem, to be sung in meeting, which should be read in retiring time; and none should have any conversation upon anything whatever, neither should they sleep nor idly lounge away the time, or leave the room except it be very necessary.

3. No member is allowed by the orders of God to present himself to worship him, when under the condemnation of sin unconfessed. But all are required to present themselves to worship, with clean hands, pure hearts and justified consciences.

4. All should go into meeting in the fear of God walking on their toes, and two abreast if the passage may be sufficiently wide to admit of it, keeping step together, and none should have any talking, laughing, or hanging on the railing, while going to, or coming from meeting.

5. When brethren and sisters place themselves in a body in meeting, for the worship of God, the ranks should be straight, not only to the right and left, but also forward and back; forward ranks should always be as long as the rest, and by no means should there be vacancies in the ranks, it has a tendency to excite disunion.

6. Brethren and sisters should not allow themselves to be gaping or yawning in meeting.

7. No one may be absent from meeting, without liberty from the Elders, or some other person authorised by them to give permission, and none should go out of meeting if consistent to avoid it.

8. When any person is under the operation of the power of God, or on their knees in devoted prayer, whether in meeting or elsewhere, all who are present, should attend carefully, and not be otherwise engaged.

9. Brethren and sisters may not go to each other's shops to learn songs, it has a tendency to naturalize them.

.   .   .   .   .

Section V.
Orders concerning Intercourse between the Sexes

The gospel of Christ's Second Appearing, strictly forbids all private union between the two sexes, in any case, place, or under any circumstances, in doors or out.

2. One brother and one sister, must not be together, alone, at any

time, longer than to do a short and necessary duty or errand; and must not have private talk together at all, which they desire to have unknown to the Elders. Neither should brethren and sisters touch each other unnecessarily.

3. Brethren and sisters must not work together, except on special occasions, and then by liberty from the Elders.

4. Brethren and sisters may not make presents to each other in a private manner.

5. Brethren and sisters may not write for each other nor to each other, without liberty from the Elders.

6. If brethren and sisters need instruction in reading, writing, or music, or any other branch of literature of science, they must receive it from those of their own sex, or by such persons as the Elders may appoint.

7. Brethren and sisters may not pass each other on the stairs.

8. Brethren and sisters may not shake hands together.

9. It is contrary to order for Believers to offer to shake hands with apostates; and if brethren shake hands with women of the world, or if sisters shake hands with men of the world, they must open it to their Elders before attending meeting.

10. Brethren and sisters may not go to each other's apartments, without a just and lawful occasion; but when they do go, they should rap at the door, and go in by liberty.

11. When brethren go to brethren's rooms, or sisters to sisters' rooms, they should ask if they may come in, but this is not the order or duty of Ministry or Elders.

12. There must not be any sitting or standing on the outside steps, railings or platforms, nor in the doors, or halls to hold lengthy conversations, either of brethren with brethren, sisters with sisters, or of brethren and sisters together.

13. Brethren and sisters must not go into each other's apartments, after evening meeting at night, except on some very needful occasion.

14. The brethren must all leave their rooms, while the sisters are doing the necessary chores therein; unless prevented by sickness or infirmity.

15. Sisters must not mend, nor set buttons on brethren's clothes, while they have them on.

16. Sisters should not use cloths that have their own initials on to

do up brethren's clothes in, nor keep the brethren's clothes with their's, neither hang them side by side, nor together.

17. Brethren and sisters must not wear each other's clothes, nor be trying them on, on any occasion whatever.

18. When brethren and sisters come together to support union, their conversation should be open and general, and no whispering or blinking may be done at such times; and blinking should never be practised.

19. None should sit crosslegged nor in any awkward posture, in the time of any meeting for worship; and in union, or singing meeting there should be at least five feet distance, between the seats of brethren and sisters, when there is sufficient room to admit of it.

20. No fans, cologne water, or any kind of perfumery, may be used in time of union meetings, or any other meeting, neither should any one or ones, scent themselves with perfumes, immediately before attending such meetings.

21. All are required to attend union meetings at the appointed times, unless special duty requires them to be absent; and such absence should be by liberty of the Elders. Real flesh hunters, are generally willing to be absent from an orderly union meeting, and to meet their peculiar favorites in private.

22. None should leave union meetings, or any meetings for worship, only on necessary duties, which should seldom occur, requiring such absence.

23. Brethren's and sister's shops, should not be under one and the same roof, except those of the Ministry.

24. When sisters walk out into the fields, to the barns, or out buildings, or even to the brethren's shops, there should be at least two in company.

.   .   .   .   .

Section VI.
Orders concerning the Language of Believers

Believers are not allowed to call nicknames, or use bywords, not to call each other by the last name, adding the title of doctor, friend, etc.

2. No Believer should ever repeat the cursing and swearing of the world, when relating any circumstance, or telling stories.

3. Believers should never use vulgar expressions, like the following, viz. I wish I was dead! I wish I could die! I wish I had never been born! My Stars! Good heavens! My gracious! etc. or any thing of the like nature, it is wicked.

4. Believers should not use rough, vulgar words, nor tell light, vain, nonsensical stories which are known to be untrue.

5. All filthy stories, and all conversation which tends to excite lustful sensations, are directly contrary to the purity of the gospel, and utterly forbidden. And whoever offends in this manner, must make confession before meeting, or stand behind all in the ranks, when assembled for worship. All who hear or listen to any such story or conversation, are required to open it before meeting.

6. It is contrary to order, for any Believer to blend with the world in conversation upon politics, jesting, joking or talking upon any thing that will serve to draw the sense from the pure way of God.

7. All telling of falsehood, evil speaking one of an other, backbiting or tattling, are utterly forbidden by the gospel.

8. No one should carry news, from one to an other, that will stir up and make mischief; or bring up faults and failing that have been confessed and put away. Neither should the mistakes and missteps of any one, either those in the body or out, be handed down from generation to generation.

9. It is ungodly for brethren and sisters to talk of rejecting their privilege among Believers, or in the way of God, and of falling back to the world.

5. A Day with the Shakers

Charles Lane, a member of Brook Farm, published this sympathetic account of Shaker life after a visit in 1843.

Between two and three miles northward of the centre village in the township of Harvard, Massachusetts, the traveller discerns a rustic guide board, on which is inscribed "To the Shaker Village."

"A Day with the Shakers," *Dial,* October, 1843, pp. 165–68.

Uncouth name for any association of serious people seriously to adopt; yet we never hear them called otherwise. The Quakers, we all know, denominate themselves "the Society of Friends," but these people seem to have no other appellation besides this grotesque one thus placed at the road's head: Possibly, however, the town erected the board, and they did not originate the popular and current designation of themselves.

At about half a mile up this road we arrive at three of four houses of no very attractive exterior, with a large stone barn, having very much the appearance of a prison, which for the animals contained therein probably it is. At this station, which is the probationary village for such persons as propose to join the family, the visitor is met by some of the brethren, amongst whom will be found one of superior intelligence, who in good temper answers questions to which he has probably responded some hundreds of times before. Most likely the conversation turns upon the subject of self-denial, and thence naturally to their especial instance of it, that is to say abstinence from marriage. Of him you may learn that the number in the family is about two hundred persons, of whom only thirty-eight are under sixteen years of age, and not one is younger than four; that they did not settle here from any choice of this rough and sterile domain of about fifteen hundred acres, but because their founder, Ann Lee, received from the persons who resided here during her brief earthly sojourn that cordial support and sympathy which frequently attends the career of the pious.

Passing this group of buildings, on a turn of the road to the left hand over a broad slab of rock, a street of houses is presented to the view. Some of these buildings are small and old; some are large and new. Many active laborers are in the fields and gardens, and improvements are carried on with vigor; but there is much to be done, by reason of the original rudeness of this spot, in order to bring the external appearances to a like elevation with that which common report has assigned to other stations. The orchards and gardens are the most striking achievements, and this family trades extensively in seeds.

No formal introduction is required; on the contrary, there is a general disposition on the part of both the more intelligent men and women to enter into free conversation at once upon their distinguishing practice of self-sacrifice. On the subject of abstinence from outward marriage they are as lively and energetic as recent converts. It reigns so monarchically in their hearts that they have always a stirring topic whereon to speak, and an exalting object for which to act. So far from being lifeless or indifferent about other persons, they seem to be fully aware that unless fresh comers are gathered in from the world at large, their family must decline gradually to total extinction. There is, therefore, great promptness manifested in laying their arguments before sincere inquirers, although they are not so zealous as to send forth especial missionary brethren. Words alone they may perhaps consider would be fruitless; while in conjunction with a life fully realizing them, they become almost irresistible. The family being thus sustained by the addition of convinced minds, and not by the imposition of educative habits, there will probably be ever found a degree of animation and heartfelt zeal unknown amongst other religious orders.

Our business being the purchase of a few seeds, and the gardener being occupied out of doors, the trading agent attended us to the store, and supplied the articles with an activity and business intelligence, which prove him qualified to conduct any such transactions they may have with the old world. Their trade, he informed us, amounts generally to the large sum of ten thousand dollars a year. For persons of simple habits, desirous of relief from circumstances morally depressive, this is far too great an involvement in money affairs; but it seems to grow out of their peculiar position, and the want of true simplicity in many particulars. Their estate does not at present produce a full supply of bread-corn; most of the members, except the children, consume flesh-meat; much milk is used; and the aged amongst them still drink tea, or coffee, and the like. For these reasons some of their produce has to be exchanged, which occasions considerable traffic. To provide for their wants they also are extensive manufacturers of various clothing and other fabrics, and have to buy raw material to work upon, as well as to sell the goods when finished. These proceedings require more extensive interchanges of money, and more frequent intercourse with the world, than seems compatible with a serene life.

Yet their life is serene. The repose, quiet, and cleanliness reigning throughout the establishment are indeed as remarkable as attractive.

As a retreat for the thoughtful or poetic mind, it seems most desirable. You could there "walk gowned," conscious of feelings as reverential as those which pervade the bosom of the worshipper when he enters the ancient cathedral. Nor is the superstition there, nor the outward devotion which results from the artistic effects of architecture, painting, music, and the rest. Of these they can boast none. As they have built several spacious houses for themselves, their idea has necessarily been expressed by an architecture of some character, yet wanting in most or all of those artifices which distinguish edifices erected by other religionists. The building last erected is large and plain. Externally it has somewhat the appearance of a school-house or church. Internally, however, it is divided into separate apartments, and is of several stories. Corridors in the middle, with rooms on each side, keep the whole well-ventilated, light and cheerful. The stairs and most of the floors being covered with a homemade carpet, the foot-tread is inaudible. At this house visitors are received and entertained; and if they remain during a meal time, here take their repast; the accommodations being reported too small to permit even all the inmates to eat together. The internal fittings of the new house are of the most comfortable kind. Window-sashes, spring-blinds, closets, &c. are of the best workmanship and most convenient contrivances for endurance. The joinery is not painted, but varnished slightly, so that it can be cleaned with facility; and the only objection seems to be the use of close stoves instead of open fire-places. The furniture is not home-made, but is wrought mostly in a more ancient fashion still common to the country, and much more cheap than elegant or luxurious.

New Jerusalem

Influenced by the revival fervor of the New Light Baptists and the celibate doctrines of Ann Lee, Jemima Wilkinson (1752–1819) gathered about her a colony named New Jerusalem in Yates County, New York. During the course of a fever in 1776 she fell into a 36-hour trance and afterwards announced that her soul had died. Henceforth she called herself "The Publick Universal Friend" and, with her new soul, traveled throughout Rhode Island, Massachusetts, and Connecticut preaching celibacy, equality of the sexes, and modified communism.

By all accounts she was a gentle, handsome woman capable of exerting a great personal influence over the family that settled near her. When Liancourt, the Duke de la Rochefoucauld, visited her in 1796 her settlement was prosperous and her family consisted of over 260 individuals living in private dwellings surrounding "The Friends" house. After her death in 1819 the community disintegrated, but as late as 1848 there were still 200 members, though only a few were practicing celibacy.

Her colony was a forerunner of the Owenite and Fourierist experiments and complemented the Shakers' work in announcing the community way to the "burned-over" district of western New York.

6. Visit by the Duc de La Rochefoucauld

We saw Jemima, and attended her meeting, which is held in her own house. We found there about thirty persons, men, women, and children. Jemima stood at the door of her bed-chamber on a carpet, with an arm-chair behind her. She had on a white morning gown, and waistcoat, such as men wear, and a petticoat of the same colour. Her black hair was cut short, carefully combed, and divided behind into three ringlets; she wore a frock, and a white silk cravat, which was tied about her neck with affected negligence. In point of delivery, she preached with more ease, than any other Quaker, I have yet heard; but the subject matter of her discourse was an eternal repetition of the same topics, death, sin, and repentance. She is said to be about forty years of age, but she did not appear to be more than thirty. She is of middle stature, well made, of a florid countenance, and has fine teeth, and beautiful eyes. Her action is studied; she aims at simplicity, but there is somewhat of pedantic in her manner. In her chamber we found her friend, Rachel Miller, a young woman of about twenty-eight or thirty years of age, her follower and admirer, who is entirely devoted to her. All the land which Jemima possesses is purchased in the name of Rachel Miller, an advantage which she owes to her influence over her adherents, and to her dexterity in captivating their affections.

Jemima, or *the Friend* (as she is called by way of eminence) inculcates, as her leading tenet, poverty, and resignation of all earthly possessions. If you talk to her of her house, she always calls it "the house, which I inhabit." This house, however, though built only of the trunks of trees, is extremely pretty and commodious. Her room is exquisitely neat; and resembles more the *boudoir* of a fine lady, than the cell of a nun. It contains a looking glass, a clock, an arm-chair, a good bed, a warming-pan, and a silver saucer. Her garden is kept in good order; her spring-house is full of milk, cheese, butter, butcher's-meat and game. Her hypocrisy may be traced in all her discourses, actions, and conduct, and even in the very manner in

Francois Alexandre Frederic, Duc de La Rochefoucauld-Liancourt, *Travels throughout the United States of North America* (London, 1799), pp. 112–20.

which she manages her countenance. She seldom speaks, without quoting the Bible, or introducing a serious sentence about death, and the necessity of making our peace with God. Whatever does not belong to her own sect is with her an object of distaste and stedfast aversion. She sows dissention in families, to deprive the lawful heir of his right of inheritance, in order to appropriate it to herself; and all this she does under the name and by the agency of her companion, who receives all the presents brought by the faithful, and preserves them for her *reverend friend,* who, being wholly absorbed in her communion with Christ, whose prophetess she is, would absolutely forget the supply of her bodily wants, if she were not well taken care of. The number of her votaries has, of late, much decreased. Many of the families, who followed her to Jerusalem, are no longer the dupes of her self-interested policy. Some still keep up the outward appearance of attachment to her; while other have openly disclaimed their connexion with Jemima. Such however as still continue her adherents, appear to be entirely devoted to her. With these she passes for a prophetess, an indescribable being; she is not Jemima Wilkinson, but a spirit of a peculiar name, which remains a profound secret to all, who are not true believers; she is the *Friend,* the *All-friend.* Six or seven girls of different ages, but all young and handsome, wait upon her, with surprising emulation, to enjoy the peculiar satisfaction of being permitted to approach this celestial being. Her fields, and her garden, are ploughed and dug by the Friends, who neglect their own business, to take care of her's; and the *All-friend* is so condescending, as not to refuse their services; she comforts them with a kind word now and then, makes enquiries after and provides for their health and welfare, and has the art of effectually captivating their affections, the more perhaps because she knows how to keep her votaries at a respectful distance.

When the service was over, Jemima invited us to dinner. The hope of watching her more narrowly induced us to accept the invitation; but we did not then know, that it forms a part of the character she acts, never to eat with any one. She soon left us; and locking herself up with her female friend, sat down, without other company, to an excellent dinner; we did not get ours, till after she had dined. When our dinner was over, and also another, which was served up after ours, the sanctuary opened again. And now Jemima appeared once more at the door of her room, and conversed with us, seated in an arm-chair. When strangers are with her, she never comes over the threshold of her bedroom; and when by herself, she is constantly engaged in deliberation how to improve the demesne of her friend. The house was, this day, very full. Our company consisted of exactly ten persons; after us dined another company of the same number; and as many dined in the kitchen. Our plates, as well as the table-linen, were perfectly clean and neat; our repast, although frugal, was yet better in quality than any, of which we had partaken, since our departure from Philadelphia; it consisted of good fresh meat, with pudding, an excellent sallad, and a beverage of a peculiar yet charming flavour, with which we were plentifully supplied out of Jemima's apartment, where it was prepared. The devout guests observed, all this while, a profound silence; they either cast down their eyes, or lifted them up to heaven with a rapturous sigh; to me they appeared, not unlike a party of the faithful, in the primitive ages, dining in a church.

The *All-friend* had by this time exchanged her former dress for that of a fine Indian lady, which, however, was cut out in the same fashion as the former. Her hair and eye-brows had again been combed. She did not utter a syllable respecting our dinner; nor did she offer to make any apology for her absence. Constantly engaged in personating the part she has assumed, she descanted in a sanctimonious, mystic tone, on death, and on the happiness of having been a useful instrument to others in the way of their salvation. She afterwards gave us a rhapsody of prophecies to read, ascribed to one Dr. Love, who was beheaded in Cromwell's time; wherein she clearly discerned, according to her accounts, the French Revolution, the decline and downfall of Popery, and the impending end of the world. Finding, however, that this conversation but ill adapted to engage our attention, she cut short her harangue at once. We had indeed already seen more than enough, to estimate the character of this bad actress, whose pretended sanctity only inspired us with contempt and disgust, and who is altogether incapable of imposing upon any person of common understanding, unless those of the most simple minds, or downright enthusiasts. Her speeches are so strongly contradicted by the the tenor of her actions; her whole conduct, her expence, compared with that of other families, within a circumference of fifty miles, her way of living, and her dress, form such a striking contrast with her harangues on the subject of contemning earthly enjoyments; and the extreme assiduity, with which she is continually endeavouring to induce children, over whom she has any influence, to leave their parents, and form a part of her community; all those particulars so strongly militate against the doctrine of peace and universal love, which she is incessantly preaching, that we were actually struck with abhorrence of her duplicity and hypocrisy, as soon as the first emotions of our curiosity subsided.

Her fraudulent conduct, indeed, has been discovered by so many persons, and so much has been said against it, that it is difficult to account for her having had any adherents at all, even for a short time. And yet she will probably retain a sufficient number, to encrease still further her fortune, which is already considerable for the country in which she resides, and fully adequate to the only end which she seems anxious to attain; namely, to live independent, in a decent, plentiful, and even elegant manner. There are so many weak-minded religionists, and Jemima is so particularly careful to select her disciples among persons who are either very old or very young, that her imposture, however gross and palpable to the discerning, may yet be carried on for some time with success, sufficient to answer her ultimate purpose. If her credit should sink too low, she would find herself constrained to transplant her holiness to some other region; and, in fact, she had, last year, harboured the design of removing her family and establishment, and of settling in Carlton Island, on the Lake of Ontario, where she would enjoy the satisfaction of living under the English Government, which, by her account, has proffered her a grant of land.

If we may believe common rumour, she dissuades the young women generally from marrying. In regard to those about her, this advice originates from motives of personal interest. I have little doubt, but that the pious devotion of these girls is fervent enough, to submit to all the caprices of the *All-friend* (which in their belief are inspirations). Another report is also handed about, that she has met with a male being, whom she fancies sufficiently purified, to unite occasionally with her own exalted society and converse. On this head a story prevails, which, though somewhat ludicrous, may yet properly find a place in a work of the gravest complexion, especially as it affords an additional proof of the endless muliplicity of pious deceptions.

Among other votaries of Jemima was one '*Squire* Parker, who settled in her neighbourhood, and still resides near Friendsmill. Though a jolly fellow, ever gay and jocund, he espoused very zealously the cause and interest of the prophetess. This Parker, who was constantly in Jemima's retinue, gave himself out to be the Prophet Elijah, and very rightly conceived, that, by assuming a peculiar dress, he should give a more imposing character to his impostures. He wore accordingly a white gown with large sleeves, and a girdle; in short, whatever he fancied might belong to the costume of the ancient prophets. This was the being, who was honoured with the high privilege of living with the *All-friend* on terms of the greatest intimacy. One evening the 'Squire, during a colloquy, instituted by the divine and holy friend for the edification of her flock, stole into the celestial bed, which happened to be already occupied by a young girl of only fourteen. This girl, who had frequently heard the *All-friend* say, that the Messiah sometimes appeared to her in her bed under different forms, and that she then conversed with him, fancied herself chosen by heaven to enjoy the felicity of being a witness of one of these apparitions, and retired piously to the edge of the bed, where with awful respect and in profound silence she listened to the repeated raptures, with which the pretended Messiah blessed the *All-friend.* The next morning the poor girl could not refrain from indulging her vanity by acquainting all her friends, that in the bed of her *friend* she had seen Christ, but who greatly resembled, she said, the Prophet Elijah. Her curious and enraptured friends enquired into all the particulars of this apparition, of which she gave the most satisfactory and circumstantial account in her power. It will hardly be doubted, that this religious trick not a little strengthened the credulity of the female friends in the *All-friend,* and inspired Jemima with assurance, frequently to enjoy similar apparitions.

A justice of the peace in the country, speaking of Jemima, assured us also, that one of the girls, who lived with her, has judicially deposed, that, one day, she heard the cry of a new-born infant, which Jemima's negro-woman, as is conjectured, was in the act of smothering between two mattresses. That this deposition exists is undeniable; but the fact itself is so atrocious, that it would seem incredible with respect to any other person except a prophetess. Whether this child were the result of a flip of one of the maids of honour, or the fruit of her own intercourse with the apparitions, is not known. If, from the little regard that has been paid to this story, its veracity should appear doubtful, let it be observed, that in this new country justice is but seldom duly administered; that, often, it is difficult to obtain it at all; and that no one deems himself interested in substantiating the truth of the deposition, which, after all, it would be no easy matter to do. Dervises, pontiffs, and priests of most religious persuasions throughout the world, such at least as would render religion subservient to worldly purposes, are either impostors or enthusiasts. Alas! alas! much the greater number, I fear, belong with Jemima to the former class!

The first settlers, who thoughtlessly followed their divinity to this place, not being able to purchase the lands, which composed the three districts, the remainder has been restored to the company, who have again disposed of it, and are still selling it to all, who are desirous of becoming settlers. Accordingly, numbers of Methodists, Anabaptists, and members of the Church of England, are now to be seen here; yet the colony retains its original name of *The Friends' Settlement.* Two meetings have been built here for the Quakers; one for the Methodists, and one for the Anabaptists. The soil in these parts appears to be of prime quality. The land, occupied by families of Quakers, amounts to about five hundred acres, more or less cleared, which produce excellent crops.

Pilgrims

Not all of the early groups had as long or as significant a history as the Shakers and Ephratists. Numerous small communities were started by religious enthusiasts with varying degrees of success.

The demise of the "Pilgrims" in the Arkansas territory indicates the degree to which the communal impulse moved relentlessly westward. The community, which had been organized in 1817 by Isaac Bullard, had previously settled in southern Vermont for a short time. Here is an account of their condition in 1819.

7. Timothy Flint's Travels

Before I left the country, I crossed the river to view the wretched remains of that singular class of enthusiasts, known in this country by the name of the "Pilgrims." This whole region, it is true, wears an aspect of irreligion; but we must not thence infer, that we do not often see the semblance and the counterfeit of religion. There is no country where bigotry and enthusiasm are seen in forms of more glaring absurdity, and, at the same time, of more arrogant assumption. There were, I think, six persons of them left,—the "prophet," so called, and his wife, and another woman, and perhaps three

Timothy Flint, *Recollections of the Last Ten Years* (Boston, 1826), pp. 265-71.

children. They were sick and poor; and the rags with which they were originally habited to excite attention, and to be *in keeping* with their name and assumption, were now retained from necessity. The "prophet" was too sick to impart much information, and the others seemed reluctant to do it. But from the wife of the prophet I gleaned the information which follows, of their origin, progress, and end. I have collated her information with the most authentic notices of them, which I obtained at every stage on the Mississippi where they were seen, and where they stopped.

It seems that the fermenting principle of the society began to operate in Lower Canada. A few religious people began to talk about the deadness and the unworthiness of all churches, as bodies, and they were anxious to separate from them, in order to compound a more perfect society. The enthusiasm caught in other minds like a spark fallen in flax. A number immediately sold every thing, and prepared to commence a course towards the southwest. In their progress through Vermont they came in contact with other minds affected with the same longing with themselves. There can be no doubt that most of them were perfectly honest in their purpose. The "prophet," a compound, like the character of Cromwell, of hypocrite and enthusiast, joined himself to them, and from his superior talents or contributions to the common stock of the society, became their leader. They went on accumulating through New York, where their numbers amounted to nearly fifty. Here they encountered the Shakers, and as they had some notions in common, a kind of coalition was attempted with them. But the Shakers are industrious and neat to a proverb, and are more known to the community by these traits, than any other. But industry made little part of the religion of the Pilgrims, and neatness still less, for it was a maxim with them to wear the clothes as long as they would last on the body, without washing or changing; and the more patched and particoloured the better. If they wore one whole shoe, the other one, — like the pretended pilgrims of old time, — was clouted and patched. They made it a point, in short, to be as ragged and dirty as might be. Of course, after a long debate with the Shakers, — in which they insisted upon industry, cleanliness, and parting from their wives, proving abundantly and quoting profusely that it ought to be so; and the Pilgrims proving by more numerous and apposite quotations, that they ought to cleave to their dirt, rags, laziness, and wives, and that they ought to go due southwest to find the New Jerusalem, — the logomachy terminated as most religious disputes do; each party claimed the victory, and lamented the obduracy, blindness, and certain tendency to everlasting destruction of the other; and they probably parted with these expectations of each other's doom.

I knew nothing of their course from that place to New Madrid below the mouth of the Ohio. They were then organised to a considerable degree, and had probably eight or ten thousand dollars in common stock. The prophet was their ruler, spiritual and temporal. He had visions by night, which were expounded in the morning, and determined whether they should stand still or go on; whether they should advance by land or water; in short every thing was settled by immediate inspiration. Arrived at New Madrid, they walked ashore in Indian file, the old men in front, then the women, and the children in the rear. They chanted a kind of tune, as they walked, the burden of which was "Praise God! Praise God!"

Their food was mush and milk, prepared in a trough, and they sucked it up, standing erect, through a perforated stalk of cane. They enjoined severe penances, according to the state of grace in which the penitent was. For the lower stages the penance was very severe, as to stand for four successive days without reclining or sitting, to fast one or two days. In fact fasting was a primary object of penance, both as severe in itself, and as economical. They affected to be ragged, and to have different stripes in their dresses and caps, like those adopted in penitentiaries as badges of the character of the convicts. So formidable a band of ragged Pilgrims, marching in perfect order, chanting with a peculiar twang the short phrase "Praise God! Praise God!" had in it something imposing to a people, like those of the West, strongly governed by feelings and impressions. Sensible people assured me that the coming of a band of these Pilgrims into their houses affected them with a thrill of alarm which they could hardly express. The untasted food before them lost its savour, while they heard these strange people call upon them, standing themselves in the posture of statues, and uttering only the words, "Praise God, repent, fast, pray." Small children, waggish and profane as most of the children are, were seen to shed tears, and to ask their parents, if it would not be fasting enough, to leave off one meal a day. Two of their most distinguished members escaped from them at New Madrid, not without great difficulty, and having been both of them confined to prevent their escape. One of them, an amiable and accomplished woman, whose over-wrought imagination had been carried away by their imposing rites, died soon after, worn down by the austerities and privations which she had endured. The husband had an emaciated look, like the Shakers, a sweet voice for sacred music, and was preaching in union with the Methodists. At Pilgrim Island, thirty miles below, and opposite the Little Prairie, they staid a long time.

Here dissensions began to spring up among them. Emaciated with hunger, and feverish from the filth and the climate, many of them left their bones. They were ordered by the prophet, from some direct revelation which he received, to lie unburied; and their bones were bleaching on the island when we were there. Some escaped from them at this place, and the sheriff of the county of New Madrid, indignant at the starvation imposed as a discipline upon the little children, carried to them a pirogue of provisions, keeping off with his sword the leaders, who would fain have prevented these greedy innocents from satiating their appetites.

While on this island, a great number of boatmen are said to have joined, to take them at their profession of having no regard for the world, or the things of it, and robbed them of all their money, differently stated to be between five and ten thousand dollars. From this place, reduced in number by desertion and death, in their descent to the mouth of the Arkansas, there were only the numbers surviving, which I saw. When I asked the wife of the prophet, why, instead of descending in the summer to the sickly country, they had not ascended to the high and healthy regions of Cape Girardeau, in order to acclimate themselves before their descent; their answer was, that such calculations of worldly wisdom were foreign to their object; that they did not study advantage, or calculate to act as the world acts upon such subjects, but that suffering was a part of their plan. When I asked them, why they deserted their station at the mouth of the Arkansas on the Mississippi; they answered, that they could neither get corn, pumpkins, nor milk, at the mouth of the river, as the people there had neither fields nor cows; that they could obtain all these things in the region where they were, and had come thither for this purpose. When I observed to them that this was reasoning precisely of a character with that, which I had been recommending to them, in respect to ascending the river to Cape Girardeau, and that, unknown to themselves, they were acting upon the universal principle of attempting to better their condition; they discovered that they had committed themselves, and had proved, that they acted from motives contrary to their avowed principles, and replied, that they were not used to such discussions, and that they reasoned as differently from the world, as they acted. This history of the delusion, and destruction of between thirty and forty people, most of them honest and sincere, left a deep and melancholy impression of the universal empire of bigotry, and its fatal influences in all ages and countries. To this narrative I shall only add, that I heard an aged man, with a long beard, preaching, as they called it, at New Madrid. He descended the Mississippi a year after these unfortunate people, and he also called himself a Pilgrim. He was as wild and visionary as they were, and talked and acted like a maniac. He was descending the Mississippi, as he said, to the *real* Jerusalem in Asia. He appeared deeply impressed, that by going on in that direction he should finally reach that city. There was a numerous audience, and I heard many of them expressing their admiration of his preaching. Let none think that the age of fanaticism has gone by.

Owenism

The work of Robert Owen (1771-1858) and his abortive colony at New Harmony, Indiana, is central to the communitarian tradition in America. It was Owen with his secular rationalism who provided a link between the chiliasm of the 18th century and the liberal political progressives of the 19th. As a young man he amassed a considerable fortune as manager and operator of the New Lanark, Scotland, mills, which he ran on a basis that was both profitable and humane.

In his *New View of Society* (1814) he argued that "the character of man, is, without a single exception formed for him." Owen spent his life setting down guidelines that would practically arrange a material climate for happiness. New Lanark was a mill town of 2,000 that Owen saw in collective rather than economic terms. He established schools for the workers and their children, sanitary working conditions, and a social center. In 1817 he turned his attention away from his industrial experiment toward the larger world in need of reform. He lectured and wrote widely, always in the hope that the nation's leaders would recognize the necessity for a new moral order based on principles of enlightened self-interest and scientific analysis.

In the fall of 1824 Owen journeyed to America in order to put his social and economic theories into practice. He spoke before the Congress in February, 1825, and was received by the leading men of the republic. With the purchase of land and buildings from the Rappites – they moved back to Penn-

sylvania—the New Harmony community came into being.
Within three years it was a shambles as dissident groups
fought and their leaders clashed. Owen sold his interest in the
society.

8. Robert Owen Letter — 1817

Prior to his first public discussion of a scheme for the new
society, Owen placed a series of letters in the London newspapers. In the following letter he spells out the evils of the
industrial towns and suggests some alternatives for a new village
system.

August 7th, 1817

MR. EDITOR,

SIR,—Strict justice to the public renders it necessary that my
sentiments and views should be fully and fairly before it, prior to the
Meeting to be held at the City of London Tavern, at Twelve
o'Clock, on Thursday next, the 14th instant. Your early insertion,
therefore, of the following, will confer a favour on,

Sir, your obliged,

R. OWEN

49, CHARLOTTE STREET, PORTLAND PLACE.

*A Sketch of some of the Errors and Evils arising from the Past
and Present State of Society, with an Explanation of some of the
peculiar advantages to be derived from the Arrangement of the
Unemployed Working Classes into "Agricultural and Manufacturing Villages of Unity and Mutual Cooperation," limited to a
Population of from 500 to 1,500 Persons.*

To enable the public more easily to comprehend the subject, it is
necessary to begin with first principles.

_____

"Letter to London Newspapers, August 7, 1817" *A Supplementary Ap-
pendix to the First Volume of The Life of Robert Owen, Containing a Series
of Reports, Addresses, Memorials, and Other Documents* (London, 1967).

The object of all human exertions is to be happy.

Happiness cannot be attained, enjoyed, and secured, unless all men possess health, real knowledge, and wealth.

Hitherto health and real knowledge have been neglected for the attainment of wealth and other exclusive individual objects; but which, when acquired, even in the greatest profusion, have been, and ever will be, found to destroy happiness.

The world is now saturated with wealth—with inexhaustible means of still increasing it—and yet misery abounds! Such at this moment is the actual state of human society. No arrangement, proceeding from a defined intention to attain an object of desire, could be worse devised than that which is now in practice throughout all the nations of the earth. Immense, invaluable energies, competent with ease to procure everything beneficial to humanity, lie waste, or are so misdirected as to defeat the object of all their wishes.

The world, however, is now amply supplied with the means to stop the current of human folly, to call those dormant powers into action, and to give a right straightforward direction to all the energies of man.

The means are wanted to give health, real knowledge, and wealth, to all men.

The means surround us, are at our instant disposal, and exist in a superfluity of abundance; yet the great mass of the world is in the depth of ignorance, without the comforts of life; a large proportion of them are in want of a sufficiency of food, subject to every privation, and are to be found at this hour in the midst of almost inconceivable distress and wretchedness.

Is the change then from the one state to the other difficult? Are there any insurmountable obstacles in the way, to prevent the accomplishment of that which is so desirable?

On the contrary, extraordinary as it may seem, the change will be most easy. No difficulty or obstacle of magnitude will be found in the whole progress. THE WORLD *knows* AND *feels* THE EXISTING EVIL; IT WILL LOOK AT THE NEW ORDER OF THINGS PROPOSED— APPROVE—WILL THE CHANGE—AND IT IS DONE.

Who, or what, shall now prevent man from being well-trained, instructed, and productively employed? Who, or what, shall now prevent him from being so trained, instructed, and employed, amidst every comfort and enjoyment, when it shall be proved, even to demonstration, that all, *without a single exception,* shall be essentially benefited by the change?

To proceed systematically in the subject, it is necessary here to state that man is by nature; what he has been made by the previous circumstances which have surrounded him; and afterwards to show what he may be made by surrounding him with new circumstances, all of which are now at the control of society.

Man, then, is born with combined propensities and qualities, differing in degree of power and in combination, sufficient to create through life individuality and distinctness of person and character.

.   .   .   .   .

We will now view man under the new circumstances in which he is about to be placed.

In the new, as under the old, he will be born in ignorance.

He will be trained from earliest infancy to acquire only kind and benevolent dispositions.

He will be taught facts only. These will enable him very early in life to understand clearly how his own character and the character of his fellow-creatures have been formed and are forming. He will thus be secured from being enveloped by any of the evil and demoralising atmospheres with which every man yet born has been surrounded.

No circumstances will exist to compel him to acquire feelings of disunion and separation from any other human being. On the contrary, his heart will be open to receive, and his hand ready to assist, each of his fellow creatures, whatever may be his sect, his class, his party, his country, or his colour. Anger, hatred, and revenge, will have no place on which to rest: the pabulum on which all the evil passions fed, will no longer exist: unity and mutual co-operation, to any extent, will become easy of execution, and the common practice of all.

Men will soon read their past history, only to retain a remembrance of the errors and inconsistencies from whence they emerged; and to compare the happiness around them with the misery of former times.

Look now at the drawing exhibited, and compare the scenes which it but faintly represents, with the situation of the existing poor and working classes in the manufacturing towns; and yet the ex-

pense and trouble of the latter are tenfold those of the one represented.

We will very hastily and slightly sketch the contrast.

In the Manufacturing Towns, — the poor and working classes now usually live in garrets or cellars, within narrow lanes or confined courts.

In the Proposed Villages, — the poor and working classes will live in dwellings formed into a large square, rendered in every way convenient, and usefully ornamented.

In the Manufacturing Towns, — they are surrounded with dirt, enveloped in smoke, and have seldom a pleasant object on which to fix their eye.

In the Proposed Villages, — they will be surrounded by gardens, have abundance of space in all directions to keep the air healthy and pleasant: they will have walks and plantations before them, within the square, and well cultivated grounds, kept in good order around, as far as the eye can reach.

In the Manufacturing Towns, — parents are oppressed with anxiety to secure the means of subsistence for themselves and children.

In the Proposed Villages, — in consequence of the principle of mutual co-operation being understood and practiced to its full extent, the necessaries and comforts of life are enjoyed by all in abundance.

In the Manufacturing Towns, — each family has the care and trouble of going to market to supply their individual wants, and under every disadvantage.

In the Proposed Villages, — the same trouble will provide for 1000 as is now required for one family; and all articles will be procured on the best terms.

In the Manufacturing Towns, — each family must have domestic arrangements for cooking, &c., and one person must be wholly occupied in preparing provisions, &c., for a family of ordinary numbers.

In the Proposed Villages, — the best provisions will be cooked in the best manner, under arrangements that will enable five or six individuals to prepare provisions for 1000.

In the Manufacturing Towns, — the parents must toil from ten to sixteen hours in the day to procure the wretched subsistence which they obtain for themselves and children, and very often under circumstances the most unfavourable to health and natural enjoyments.

In the Proposed Villages, — the parents will be healthfully and pleasantly occupied not more than eight hours in the day.

In the Manufacturing Towns, — in bad times, and which frequently occur, the parties experience a distress not easily to be described.

In the Proposed Villages, — no bad time can occur from a change of markets, or from any commercial uncertainties, as the parties will always have a plentiful stock of all things necessary.

In the Manufacturing Towns, — in cases of sickness, every evil takes place among these individualised beings.

In the Proposed Villages, — in the event of sickness, the utmost attention and care will be experienced: every one, both from principle and interest, will be active and have pleasure in rendering the situation of the invalid as comfortable as possible.

In the Manufacturing Towns, — the early death of parents leaves the children orphans, and subject to every evil.

In the Proposed Villages, — the early death of parents leaves the children in all respects well provided for and protected.

In the Manufacturing Towns, — the children are usually sickly, and, as well as their parents, ill-clothed.

In the Proposed Villages, — the children will be ruddy and healthy, and, as well as their parents, neat, clean, and properly clothed.

In the Manufacturing Towns, — the young children are much neglected, and hourly acquire bad habits.

In the Proposed Villages, — the children will be well looked after, prevented from acquiring bad, and taught good, habits.

In the Manufacturing Towns,— the education of the children is neglected.

In the Proposed Villages, — the children all well trained and well informed.

In the Manufacturing Towns, — the children sent early in life to some one trade or manufacture, usually of a very unhealthy nature, and at which they must attend from ten to sixteen hours per day.

In the Proposed Villages, — the children gradually instructed in gardening, agriculture, and some trade or manufacture, and only employed according to age and strength.

In the Manufacturing Towns, — the children trained under ignorant persons, possessing many bad habits.

In the Proposed Villages, — the children will be trained by intelligent persons, possessing only good habits.

In the Manufacturing Towns,— scolding, coercion, and punishments, are the usual instruments of training.

In the Proposed Villages,— kindness and good sense will be the only instruments of training.

To proceed with the contrast would be endless; the mind of the reader will easily supply the remainder: suffice it therefore to say —

That the Manufacturing Towns are the abode of poverty, vice, crime, and misery.

While the Proposed Villages will ever be the abode of abundance, active intelligence, correct conduct, and happiness.

9. History of New Harmony

John H. Noyes, the founder of the Oneida Community, used A. J. Macdonald's manuscript to reconstruct a short history of New Harmony for his *History of American Socialisms*. Mac-

John H. Noyes, *History of American Socialisms* (Philadelphia, 1870), pp. 34–42.

donald had been interested in Owenism in Scotland and collected much of his information on a visit to New Harmony in 1842. He died before he was able to put the material in book form and it was not until 1870 that Noyes made use of the material.

Quoted sections are Macdonald's own words; unquoted sections are Noyes's condensations of Macdonald's material.

OWEN'S NEW HARMONY

"Robert Owen came to the United States in December 1824, to complete the purchase of the settlement at Harmony. Mr. Rapp had sent an agent to England to dispose of the property, and Mr. Owen fell in with him there. In the spring of 1825 Mr. Owen closed the bargain. The property consisted of about 30,000 acres of land; nearly 3,000 acres under cultivation by the society; 19 detached farms; 600 acres of improved land occupied by tenants; some fine orchards; eighteen acres of full-bearing vines; and the village, which was a regularly laid out town, with streets running at right angles to each other, and a public square, around which were large brick edifices, built by the Rappites for churches, schools, and other public purposes."

We can form some idea of the size of the village from the fact which we learn from Mr. Williams; that the Rappites, while at Harmony, numbered one thousand souls. It does not appear from Macdonald's account that Owen and his Community made any important additions to the village.

"On the departure of the Rappites, persons favorable to Mr. Owen's views came flocking to New Harmony (as it was thenceforth called) from all parts of the country. Tidings of the new social experiment spread far and wide; and, although it has been denied, yet it is undoubtedly true, that Mr. Owen in his public lectures invited the 'industrious and well disposed of all nations' to emigrate to New Harmony. The consequence was, that in the short space of six weeks from the commencement of the experiment, a population of eight hundred persons was drawn together, and in October 1825, the number had increased to nine hundred."

As to the character of this population, Macdonald insists that it was "as good as it could be under the circumstances," and he gives the names of "many intelligent and benevolent individuals who were at various times residents at New Harmony." But he admits that there were some "black sheep" in the flock. "It is certain," he says, "that there was a proportion of needy and idle persons, who crowded in to avail themselves of Mr. Owen's liberal offer; and that they did their share of work more in the line of *destruction* than *construction*."

Constitution No. 1

On the 27th of April 1825, Mr. Owen instituted a sort of provisional government. In an address to the people in New Harmony Hall, he informed them, "that he had bought that property, and had come there to introduce the practice of the new views; but he showed them the impossibility that persons educated as they were, should change at once from an irrational to a rational system of society, and the necessity for a 'half-way house,' in which to be prepared for the new system." Whereupon he tendered them a *Constitution*, of which we find no definite account, except that it was not fully Communistic, and was to hold the people in probationary training three years, under the title of the *Preliminary Society of New Harmony*. "After these proceedings Mr. Owen left New Harmony for Europe, and the Society was managed by the *Preliminary Committee*.(!)" We may imagine, each one for himself, what the nine hundred did while Mr. Owen was away. Macdonald compiled from the *New Harmony Gazette* a very rapid but evidently defective account of the state of things in this important interval. He says nothing about the work on the 30,000 acres, but speaks of various minor businesses as "doing well." The only manufactures that appear to have "exceeded consumption" were those of soap and glue. A respectable apothecary "dispensed medicines without charge," and "the store supplied the inhabitants with all necessaries" – probably at Mr. Owen's expense. Education was considered "public property," and one hundred and thirty children were schooled, boarded and clothed from the public funds – probably at Mr. Owen's expense. Amusements flourished. The Society had a band of music; Tuesday evenings were appropriated to balls; Friday evenings to concerts – both in the old Rappite church. There was no provision for religious worship. Five military companies, "consisting of infantry, artillery, riflemen, veterans and fusileers," did duty from time to time on the public square.

Constitution No. 2

"Mr. Owen returned to New Harmony on the 12th of January, 1826, and soon after the members of the Preliminary Society held a convention, and adopted a constitution of a Community, entitled *The New Harmony Community of Equality.* Thus in less than a year, instead of three years as Mr. Owen had proposed, the 'half-way house' came to an end, and actual Communism commenced. A few of the members, who, on account of a difference of opinions, did not sign the new constitution, formed a second Community on the New Harmony estate about two miles from the town, in friendly connection with the first."

The new government instituted by Mr. Owen, was to be in the hands of an *Executive Council,* subject at all times to the direction of the Community; and six gentlemen were appointed to this function. But Macdonald says: "Difficulties ensued in organizing the new Community. It appears that the plan of government by executive council would not work, and that the members were unanimous in calling upon Mr. Owen to take the sole management, judging from his experience that he was the only man who could do so. This call Mr. Owen accepted, and we learn that soon after general satisfaction and individual contentment took the place of suspense and uncertainty."

This was in fact the inauguration of

Constitution No. 3

"In March the *Gazette* says that under the indefatigable attention of Mr. Owen, order had been introduced into every department of business, and the farm presented a scene of active and steady industry. The Society was rapidly becoming a Community of Equality. The streets no longer exhibited groups of idle talkers, but each one was busily engaged in the occupation he had chosen. The public meetings, instead of being the arenas for contending orators, were changed into meetings of business, where consultations were held and measures adopted for the comfort of all the members of the Community.

"In April there was a disturbance in the village on account of negotiations that were going on for securing the estate as private property. Some persons attempted to divide the town into several societies. Mr. Owen would not agree to this, and as he had the power, he made a selection, and by solemn examination constituted a *nucleus* of twenty-five men, which *nucleus* was to admit members, Mr. Owen reserving the power to *veto* every one admitted. There were to be three grades of members, viz., conditional members, probationary members, and persons on trial. (?) The Community was to be under the direction of Mr. Owen, until two-thirds of the members should think fit to govern themselves, provided the time was not less than twelve months."

This may be called,

Constitution No. 4

In May a third Community had been formed; and the population was divided between No. 1, which was Mr. Owen's Community, No. 2, which was called Macluria, and No. 3, which was called [*Feiba-Peveli*] — a name designating in some mysterious way the latitude and longitude of New Harmony.

"May 27. The immigration continued so steadily, that it became necessary for the Community to inform the friends of the new views that the accommodations were inadequate, and call upon them by advertisement not to come until further notice."

Constitution No. 5

"May 30. In consequence of a variety of troubles and disagreements, chiefly relating to the disposal of the property, a great meeting of the whole population was held, and it was decided to form four separate societies, each signing its own contract for such part of the property as it should purchase, and each managing its own affairs; but to trade with each other by paper money."

Mr. Owen was now beginning to make sharp bargains with the independent Communities. Macdonald says, "He had lost money, and no doubt he tried to regain some of it, and used such means as he thought would prevent further loss."

On the 4th of July Mr. Owen delivered his celebrated *Declaration of Mental Independence,* from which we give the following specimen:

"I now declare to you and to the world, that Man, up to this hour, has been in all parts of the earth a slave to a Trinity of the most monstrous evils that could be combined to inflict mental and physical evil upon his whole race. I refer to Private or Individual Property, Absurd and Irrational systems of Religion, and Marriage founded on Individual Property, combined with some of these Irrational systems of Religion."

"August 20. After Mr. Owen had given his usual address, it was unanimously agreed by the meeting that the entire population of New Harmony should meet three times a week in the Hall, for the purpose of being educated together. This practice was continued about six weeks, when Mr. Owen became sick and it was discontinued."

Constitution No. 6

"August 25. The people held a meeting at which they *abolished all officers* then existing, and appointed three men as *dictators.*"

Constitution No. 7

"Sept. 17. A large meeting of all the Societies and the whole population of the town took place at the Hall, for the purpose of considering a plan for the *'amelioration of the Society,* to improve the condition of the people, and make them more contented.' A message was received from Mr. Owen proposing to form a Community with as many as would join him, and put in all their property, save what might be thought necessary to reserve to help their friends; the government to consist of Robert Owen and four others of his choice, to be appointed by him every year; and not to be altered for five years. This movement of course nullified all previous organizations. Disagreements and jealousies ensued, and, as was the case on a former change being made, many persons left New Harmony.

"Nov. 1. The *Gazette* says: 'Eighteen months experience has proved to us, that the requisite qualifications for a permanent member of the Community of Common Property are, 1, Honesty of purpose; 2, Temperance; 3, Industry; 4, Carefulness; 5, Cleanliness; 6, Desire for knowledge; 7, A conviction of the fact that the character of man is formed for, and not by, himself.'

"Nov. 8. Many persons leaving. The *Gazette* shows how impossible it is for a Community of common property to exist, unless the members comprising it have acquired the genuine Community character.

Nov. 11. Mr. Owen reviewed the last six months' progress of the Community in a favorable light.

"In December the use of ardent spirits was abolished.

"Jan. 1827. Although there was an appearance of increased order and happiness, yet matters were drawing to a close. Owen was selling property to individuals; the greater part of the town was now resolved into individual lots; a grocery was established opposite the tavern; painted sign-boards began to be stuck up on the buildings, pointing out places of manufacture and trade; a sort of wax-figure-and-puppet-show was opened at one end of the boarding-house; and every thing was getting into the old style."

.   .   .   .   .

"June 18, 1827. The *Gazette* advertised that Mr. Owen would meet the inhabitants of New Harmony and the neighborhood on the following Sunday, to bid them farewell. I find no account of this meeting, nor indeed of any further movements of Mr. Owen in the *Gazette*. After his departure the majority of the population also removed and scattered about the country. Those who remained returned to individualism, and settled as farmers and mechanics in the ordinary way. One portion of the estate was owned by Mr. Owen, and the other by Mr. Maclure. They sold, rented, or gave away the houses and lands, and their heirs and assigns have continued to do so to the present day."

Hopedale

The commonplace distinction that has been made between religious and sectarian communities has disguised the fact that most communities had a great deal in common.

The Hopedale Community is a case in point. Founded by Adin Ballou, a Universalist minister, in 1842, this "fraternal community" was involved actively in antislavery, temperance, and peace activities. The members bound themselves "to abstain from murder, hatred, unchastity, use of liquor as a beverage, and all participation in military or civic affairs, including the vote."

Hopedale was a religious association that believed in the "Fatherhood of God and the brotherhood of man as taught and illustrated in the Gospel of Jesus Christ." In 1856 — 14 years after its founding — it had a membership of 110 and a joint-stock value of $40,000. It lasted until 1868.

10. Autobiography of Adin Ballou

... Twenty-eight persons were located upon the Hopedale territory before the first of April, 1842 — myself, wife, and two children among the number — all residing as a unitary household in the one dwelling house there and adjusting themselves to each other as far as

Adin Ballou, *Autobiography of Adin Ballou*, edited by William S. Heywood (Lowell, Mass., 1896), pp. 340–42.

they could, and to the unique circumstances in which they were placed. At the expiration of three weeks, when I entered upon the fortieth year of my life, domestic affairs had assumed a good degree of regularity, order, and efficiency, considering the crowded condition in which we found ourselves and the limited culinary appliances and utensils with which we had to do. My wife had been seasonably appointed director of house-keeping by the executive council, and she had for chosen assistant, our good sister, Anna T., wife of Ebenezer D. Draper. Two most excellent and capable women they were, admirably fitted for the positions they occupied, and they executed the trust reposed in them most quietly, promptly, and successfully.

Before the month closed, great progress had been made in outside matters. A practical division of industrial operations had been arranged, and each one assigned to a position of responsibility, entered upon his or her duties with commendable fidelity and earnestness. A small building, 32 feet long by 14½ wide, a story and a half high above the basement, was nearly completed — the first building erected by the Community. It contained six rooms; two on the main floor for a printing office and school, with two dormitories above and two apartments for whatever use they might be needed in the basement. A larger two-story dwelling house had been voted, but it was found that a mechanics' shop, in which a portion of our water power could be utilized, was indispensable, and that, therefore, first received attention. It was the second structure we put up and served a most important purpose in our earlier years. Our agricultural interests were judiciously provided for, the months of April and May being spent in preparing the soil and putting in the seed for an autumn harvest. When June opened we had on the farm 13 cows, 4 yokes of oxen, 2 horses, and 6 swine. We had also 17 acres of land under cultivation, and everything in this department of activity promised well for the future.

At the same time, as the weeks passed by and as our industrial and general business affairs developed, we were learning some very suggestive and valuable lessons by experience. Novelty wore off and enthusiasm cooled down. We began to see that we had undertaken more than we were aware of, and had not fully estimated our difficulties. We were greatly overcrowded by numbers, new comers frequently appearing and almost forcing themselves upon us; and as greatly pushed for want of money and means to do with. All meant well in the main, but none of us had any wisdom, strength, or patience to spare, and some of us too little of these requisite qualities for our common use. We had been led to hope for funds which did not come, and some which we had received were unexpectedly withdrawn. We had made a fine show of our plans for a new social state on paper, and had published them far and wide through the land. The rich and well-to-do derided our scheme and clutched their treasures the closer; the poor, needy, and homeless eagerly applied for a share in our privileges. Moreover, less than a third of our reliable associates had sufficient money at command to meet their own family expenses—much less to help in housing and furnishing subsisting employment to others. I, as the leader in this undertaking, ought to have been wise enough to postpone practical operations till there had been accumulated a common fund sufficient to give a comfortable home and fairly remunerative employment to those who might be enlisted under the banner of our new social state. But I was in too much haste to see the realization of my theories and plans. My hope was too large and my economic judgment too small. . . .

Regular religious meetings, two always on Sunday and sometimes three, with a social conference on Thursday evening, were established early in our Community life, and creditably sustained from week to week for many years. These were generally led by one of our approved public speakers or preachers, who usually gave a formal discourse, although in the absence of such, some layman or lay-woman, of whom there were several among us competent for the task, conducted the service. At the same time those of us who had formally entered the Christian ministry preached either statedly or occasionally at various places within a convenient distance of home, some of which we regarded as distinctive missionary stations for the inculcation and dissemination of the spirit and principles of Practical Christianity. Vigorous quarterly conferences of two or three days' continuance were held at these stations or wherever we had friends to invite us. Besides devoted attention to these religious gatherings by our ministers and people at large, we took active part in mass meetings, conventions, and celebrations held for the purpose of promoting the cause of temperance, anti-slavery, non-resistance, social reform, or whatever promised the improvement of our kind. A more industrious propaganda of regenerative religious and moral principles than this little cluster of Hopedalians existed nowhere else probably on the face of the earth.

But we labored all the while under great disadvantages, having to provide for our own material subsistence as well as for our distinctive social reform enterprise, besides helping along those other activities which have just been named. I stood in the fore front of those industries upon which we relied for means wherewith to live and lend aid to every good word and work, and though weighted down with home duties and cares, yet found time for considerable active effort abroad in behalf of truth and humanity. In October, 1843, I was chosen president of the New England Non-resistance Society, which imposed a new tax upon my time and energy. The Washingtonian Movement, which led to a conflict between the friends of moral suasion and those of legal coercion as methods of promoting the temperance reformation, and the division arising in the Abolitionist ranks upon the question of political action, both appealed to me through the issues raised, in a form and with a force which I could not wholly ignore, my feeling and conviction from the beginning being unequivocally in favor of moral and religious effort rather than legal and political, in carrying forward the work of individual and social regeneration upon the earth. I also took a decided stand and wrote against the ultra anti-Sabbatarians of those days, setting forth and promulgating what I deemed true and rational views upon the observance of the first day of the week under the Christian dispensation. The consideration of these great practical questions filled, in my thought and action, the place previously occupied by more strictly theological discussions.

Fourierism

Although the great Owenite experiment at New Harmony had failed, the communitarians did not lack further blueprints. The writings of Charles Fourier (1772- 1837), as translated and interpreted by the American journalist Albert Brisbane, provided the raw philosophy for this second great movement.

Whereas Owen had based his system of emancipation on 18th-century science and 19th-century liberalism, Fourier based his on the rejection of those benevolent virtues. For Fourier, civilized man was artificial because he had purchased his civilization at the expense of his "passional" attractions. Such notions as virtue, enlightenment, rationalism, and positivism were shams because they represented the forces of "civilization."

Fourier's critique of society emphasized the pervasive poverty of man's existence. He saw, as Frank Manuel points out, that most men were poor "because their passions are unfulfilled, their senses are not appeased, their amorous emotions are curbed, and their naturally complex social sensibilities can find outlets only in pitifully limited channels."[1] Fourier defined the passionate impulse as "the drive given us by nature prior to any reflection, persistent despite the opposition of reason, duty and prejudice." In order to encourage the development of the passions—twelve by his count—he

---

[1]Frank E. Manuel, *The Prophets of Paris* (New York: Harper Torchbooks, 1965).

constructed an elaborate social system for the 1,600-member
"phalanstery" in which work and play would be merged in
systematic fashion.

His ideas were interpreted for an American audience by
Albert Brisbane in the pages of Greeley's New York *Weekly
Tribune*. Scores of phalanxes were established throughout the
country as the reform impulse ran strong in the forties. Most
lasted for a year or less, but some—like the North American
Phalanx at Red Bank, New Jersey—had a generational life.

11. Report on Fourierism

**Fourier's scheme could not be easily summarized, but Eliza-
beth Peabody's report to the readers of *The Dial* outlined the
essential features.**

... The general view upon which Fourier proceeds is this: that
there is in the Divine Mind a certain social order, to which man is
destined, and which is discoverable by man, according to his truth in
thought to the two poles of Christian perfection, Love of God and
Love of Man.

He assumes the fact, which will hardly be disputed, that the
present social organizations are not this divine order; but that they
perpetually and necessarily generate external evils, which so com-
plicate the temptations of man, as to make innocence impossible,
and virtue only the meed of crucifixion; nor even attainable by that,
except in instances of being endowed with supernatural energy. For
the proof of this fact, he appeals to all history and all experience.

Environed, as he felt himself also to be by this extreme disorder,
yet Fourier had the courage to attempt to discover the Divine order,
and labored forty years at the work. Brought up in mercantile life,
and keeping this position, which enabled him to know personally the
customs and laws of trade, as it is; and endowed with a genius for

E. P. P., "Fourierism" *The Dial*, Vol. IV, No. 4 (April, 1844), pp.
473-83.

calculation, which, in the service of justice and benevolence, followed out the bearings of these customs and laws, and the effects of large monopolies upon the social happiness and moral character of the various men directly and indirectly affected by them; he yet, to use his own words, 'labored in distraction for seven years, before he obtained the clue.' At last, having seen that Labor stands, in the social world, for the analogous fact of motion in the physical, he pronounced the word *Attraction*, which arranged to his mind the universe of men, as once before, that same word, to a kindred genius, arranged the universe of matter.

The question then became, what is that social arrangement, so broad, and so elastic, that every man shall find, at every hour of the day, and every season of his life, *just that labor* which is to him attractive and not *repugnant*.

As Fourier places among the constituent passions of men every social charity, and even a passion for *self-sacrifice*, he could maintain that there is nothing done, and nothing to be done in the world, which might not find a willing agent, were circumstances properly arranged.

But to induce a desire for this arrangement, and evoke the ability to make it, mankind must have its scientific foundations, or harmony with the nature of things, made manifest to their reason. Man therefore must be analyzed into his constituent powers; and then the tendencies of each of these powers be studied out, and corresponding circumstances imagined, which should yield to each power its legitimate range; for such circumstances must necessarily be the Divine Order of Society to which man is destined.

Thus analyzed, man, according to Fourier, is constituted of twelve fundamental passions, consisting, firstly, of the five senses; secondly, of the four social passions, friendship, ambition, love, and the parental sentiment; and thirdly, of three intellectual powers, whose strange names, according to our best recollection, are Cabalism, Alternatism, and Emulation.

The training of these twelve powers into their appropriate activities, that each may contribute its share, both to the harmony of the Universe, and the unity of the individual, is what Fourier calls the social development of the passions.

This view of the constituency of man and the necessity of his training, may be made plainer perhaps by translating his language into that of another remarkable thinker, who seems to have had, fundamentally, the same view. Swedenborg says, that man's soul is made up of Loves, and every Love must find its Wisdom, the marriage unions of Love and Wisdom, being made manifest in Uses. The Angel of Love must find the Angel of Wisdom to whom it is betrothed, on penalty of becoming a devil, says Swedenborg. If the passions do not find their developments, by the law of groups and series, says Fourier, they become principles of disorder, and produce what we see now all around us, — *a world lying in wickedness and dead in sin.*

There is one of man's passions which has found its social development, so far as to become an illustration of the meaning of this theory with regard to all the rest; and this is the Passion of Hearing. Music is the Wisdom of this passion, and the progress of this science has involved the large variety of musical instruments, and created the song, the chorus, the opera, the oratorio, and the orchestra. So, according to Fourier, each of the senses, each of the social passions, each of the intellectual powers, in finding its legitimate scope, must create a music in its sphere, with instruments corresponding, and weave men into groups corresponding with the chorus, the opera, the oratorio, and the orchestra. And there are intimations of this. The passion of Sight has created Painting, Sculpture, Architecture. And even what seem to be the humbler powers of Touch, Taste, Smell, have not failed to bring the tribute of their exactions to the comforts and elegancies of life, and the science of vitality.

One obvious and undisputed function of the senses, is to build up bodies, and contribute to physical well-being. But this is not all. There is another function which the senses have to perform, beside this obvious one; and also beside the transcendental one of creating harmonies in five different modes; even though we may admit that all these harmonies may rise to the spiritual elevation of that divine art which Beethoven has carried to the acme of symbolizing the highest intellectual, moral, and even religious exercises of the soul. This function is to perfect the Earth on which we live, and make it not only yield its treasures for physical well-being to every creature, but perform adequately its part in the Sidereal Universe.

At this point of Fourier's system, there opens upon us a quite poetical extent of view. Geologists and geographers have intimated to us heretofore, that the earth needs to be dressed and kept by men, in order not to become in several ways desert, and that the climates, which depend much more upon the state of the surface of the earth, than upon its relations with the sun, should be ameliorated. Fourier would demonstrate that *the cursing of the ground for man's sake,* sung of by the old Hebrew prophet, is no metaphor; but that, literally, man's falling below his destiny, has, as its natural consequence, the return of the earth to a state of chaos. He demonstrates, that, following out the suggestions of the senses of taste and smell, the human race must cultivate the whole vegetable creation, if not the animal, to a perfection which would involve an agricultural science, absolutely sublime in its extent; while the spring-carriage, and easy railroad car, and every contribution the mechanical arts have made to the commodity of man, would fall among the meanest and vulgarest class of the innumerable results of seeking for the wisdom of the sense of Touch.

But is the earth to be restored to the state of Paradise, through the labors of man, merely to react upon his physical nature, and contribute to his personal enjoyments? By no means. But the earth thus cultivated and perfected, shall shine as a brighter star in the firmament of other worlds; shall hold, by its imponderable fluids, a more perfect relation with the sun, and through that star with the whole sidereal heavens.

It is hardly fair to Fourier to touch, without entering into his reasonings, upon a part of his system which is so original, and which requires, in order to be appreciated, at least all that he has himself said upon it.

If the development and training of the senses to results of science and art, have these wide bearings upon the sidereal universe, we may not doubt that Fourier makes the development and bearings of the social passions, open another captivating and exalting vista of thought.

The word Friendship, in this nomenclature, stands for the sentiment of humanity, in its widest and in its most delicate relations. Fourier attempts to show that to give this passion its scope, the social system, which is according to the divine order, will realize in its institutions all, and more than all, that declarations of the Rights of man have ever suggested; all that his hopes have aspired to and expressed, under the images of the Millennium and Fifth Monarchy.

And to balance this great liberty, the second social passion must have its scope. This passion, which he defines as the love of order, in graduating persons according to their comparative worth with relation to each other, he calls *Ambition;* thus casting out of this word its bad meaning, — for its object is no longer the exaltation of *self,* but of *worth.* It gives to every man and woman their exact place in the social scale, and justifies the idea of government. By the balance of the two passions of Friendship and Ambition, Liberty and Law will become, as they should do, the poles of a living political order.

The Passions of Love, and the Parental Sentiment, will also, when, through a general ease of circumstances, they are left free to find their legitimate exercises, dignify woman universally; and by consequence, purify the institution of marriage, and unfold the family, to their highest ends of refining, and sanctifying, and cherishing human beings, into the richest forms of life.

The Christian world, as it is, can hardly fail to acknowledge, that although Christianity has sanctified the *formula* of monogamy, yet the whole deep significance of that institution is yet to be widely appreciated. To marry from any consideration but the one of sentiment, must be considered a crime, before mankind will cease from that adultery of the heart, of which Christ warned his disciples.

Lastly, the three intellectual passions into which Fourier analyzes the Reason, have for their office to estimate the natures and ends of the foregoing nine passions, and interweave them into one web of life, according to their natures and ends; and then they will take the still higher range, of enjoying the divine order, and tracing in the happiness thence resulting, the image of God.

We see from the above rude outline, that Fourier thinks he has discovered the divine order, which is the true organization of society, by studying each of the twelve passions of man, with the same respect that the passion of hearing has been studied, in order to derive from thence the present living art of music. He thinks, that by following out the results of this study in practice, the earth would be cultivated and restored to the state of Paradise; with the superstructure thereon of a world of art, in harmony with the beauty of nature. Also, that political institutions would combine all desirable liberty, with all that can come from the observance of law, by distributing all men according to the gradation of their natures, and that individual families would be established in the purest and most powerful form; lastly, that the functions of Reason would be vindicated to their worthiest objects, of perpetually unfolding and keeping in order this great estate of man, internal and external.

If Fourier had done nothing but suggest to his race, that the divine order of society was a possible discovery, and thus have given a noble object to human investigations, and presented a worthy prize for human energy, in this direction, he would have done much. It is claimed, however, by those who have studied his works, that he has done a great deal more; that he has himself successfully worked at the practical problems; and the *Phalanx* which he has discovered in detail, is, as it were, a house already builded, into which men may go, and at once live, freed from a multitude of the evils that press upon the modern civilized state. A word or two in explanation of this Phalanx.

It is not a community of goods. It is a state of society which provides a public fund, as all societies do, and on a better security for its return in just proportions to those who produce it, but which admits of individual property as much as any partnership in trade. It is indeed a great partnership, in which the members throw in capital of three species, namely, labor, skill, and money, (which last is the representative of past labor and skill). All these species of capital will draw a large interest, when the Phalanx is in operation; but in order to prevent any great inequality of the third species of capital, (money,) it is a fundamental law of the Phalanx that small sums shall draw interest in a larger ratio than large ones. The common property, accumulated by the Phalanx in its corporate capacity, shall be subject to the will of the members, expressed by ballot and otherwise; its general destination being to provide for all children, without distinction of rank or birth, an individually appropriate education, according to their genius and capacity; also to provide public conveniences, and common comforts and amusements, and means of expressing their genius, to all the members.

The labor in the Phalanx will be organized upon scientific principles, i.e. by the law of groups and series, and individual genius and disposition will be the guide as to the distribution of the members into the several groups and series. The well being and good training of the laborer will never be sacrificed to the external object of the labor, for Fourier endeavors to demonstrate that, in the divine order, the necessity of such a sacrifice can never occur, even though all ends are answered.

Brook Farm

Brook Farm, according to Emerson, was an outgrowth of William E. Channing's "Transcendental Club" sessions. Some of the conversation led to action and the publication in October, 1841, of a statement about "A Glimpse of Christ's Idea of Society" in *The Dial*.

At the outset Brook Farm was essentially an educational association where "all labor, whether bodily or intellectual is to be paid at the same rate of wages." The original constitution spoke of Brook Farm as "a large family, including several boarding scholars, and that all work and study together." Nathaniel Hawthorne, Charles Dana, and George Ripley were among the early members. Hawthorne's disenchantment is well known through *The Blithedale Romance*.

In 1843 the West Roxbury community became a phalanx after a number of its members attended a Fourierist convention in late 1842. It was no longer solely an educational establishment, but "a regularly organized Association, embracing the various departments of industry, art and science." The community's efforts were cut short by a disastrous fire in March, 1846, which destroyed the almost completed central building – the "Phalanstery."

12. Plan of the West Roxbury Community

In the last number of the Dial were some remarks, under the
perhaps ambitious title, of "A Glimpse of Christ's Idea of Society;"
in a note to which, it was intimated, that in this number, would be
given an account of an attempt to realize in some degree this great
Ideal, by a little company in the midst of us, as yet without name or
visible existence. The attempt is made on a very small scale. A few
individuals, who, unknown to each other, under different disciplines
of life, reacting from different social evils, but aiming at the same
object, – of being wholly true to their natures as men and women;
have been made acquainted with one another, and have determined
to become the Faculty of the Embryo University.

In order to live a religious and moral life worthy the name, they
feel it is necessary to come out in some degree from the world, and
to form themselves into a community of property, so far as to
exclude competition and the ordinary rules of trade; – while they
reserve sufficient private property, or the means of obtaining it, for
all purposes of independence, and isolation at will. They have
bought a farm, in order to make agriculture the basis of their life, it
being the most direct and simple in relation to nature.

A true life, although it aims beyond the highest star, is redolent of
the healthy earth. The perfume of clover lingers about it. The lowing
of cattle is the natural bass to the melody of human voices.

On the other hand, what absurdity can be imagined greater than
the institution of cities? They originated not in love, but in war. It
was war that drove men together in multitudes, and compelled them
to stand so close, and build walls around them. This crowded condition produces wants of an unnatural character, which resulted in
occupations that regenerated the evil, by creating artificial wants.
Even when that thought of grief,

> I know, where'er I go
> That there hath passed away a glory from the Earth,

came to our first parents, as they saw the angel, with the flaming

---

"Plan of the West Roxbury Community," *The Dial*, Vol. II (January,
1842), pp. 361–65.

sword of self-consciousness, standing between them and the recovery of spontaneous Life and Joy, we cannot believe they could have anticipated a time would come, when the sensuous apprehension of Creation—the great symbol of God—would be taken away from their unfortunate children,—crowded together in such a manner as to shut out the free breath and the Universal Dome of Heaven, some opening their eyes in the dark cellars of the narrow, crowded streets of walled cities. How could they have believed in such a conspiracy against the soul, as to deprive it of the sun and sky, and glorious apparelled Earth!—The growth of cities, which were the embryo of nations hostile to each other, is a subject worthy the thoughts and pen of the philosophic historian. Perhaps nothing would stimulate courage to seek, and hope to attain social good, so much, as a profound history of the origin, in the mixed nature of man, and the exasperation by society, of the various organized Evils under which humanity groans. Is there anything, which exists in social or political life, contrary to the soul's Ideal? That thing is not eternal, but finite, saith the Pure Reason. It has a beginning, and so a history. What man has done, man may *undo*. "By man came death; by man also cometh the resurrection from the dead."

The plan of the Community, as an Economy, is in brief this; for all who have property to take stock, and receive a fixed interest thereon; then to keep house or board in commons, as they shall severally desire, at the cost of provisions purchased at wholesale, or raised on the farm; and for all to labor in community, and be paid at a certain rate an hour, choosing their own number of hours, and their own kind of work. With the results of this labor, and their interest, they are to pay their board, and also purchase whatever else they require at cost, at the warehouses of the Community, which are to be filled by the Community as such. To perfect this economy, in the course of time they must have all trades, and all modes of business carried on among themselves, from the lowest mechanical trade, which contributes to the health and comfort of life, to the finest art which adorns it with food or drapery for the mind.

All labor, whether bodily or intellectual, is to be paid at the same rate of wages; on the principle, that as the labor becomes merely bodily, it is a greater sacrifice to the individual laborer, to give his time to it; because time is desirable for the cultivation of the intellect, in exact proportion to ignorance. Besides, intellectual labor involves in itself higher pleasures, and is more its own reward, than bodily labor.

Another reason, for setting the same pecuniary value on every kind of labor, is, to give outward expression to the great truth, that all labor is sacred, when done for a common interest. Saints and philosophers already know this, but the childish world does not; and very decided measures must be taken to equalize labors, in the eyes of the young of the community, who are not beyond the moral influences of the world without them. The community will have nothing done within its precincts, but what is done by its own members, who stand all in social equality; — that the children may not "learn to expect one kind of service from Love and Goodwill, and another from the obligation of others to render it," — a grievance of the common society stated, by one of the associated mothers, as destructive of the soul's simplicity. Consequently, as the Universal Education will involve all kinds of operation, necessary to the comforts and elegances of life, every associate, even if he be the digger of a ditch as his highest accomplishment, will be an instructer in that to the young members. Nor will this elevation of bodily labor be liable to lower the tone of manners and refinement in the community. The "children of light" are not altogether unwise in their generation. They have an invisible but all-powerful guard of principles. Minds incapable of refinement, will not be attracted into this association. It is an Ideal community, and only to the ideally inclined will it be attractive; but these are to be found in every rank of life, under every shadow of circumstance. Even among the diggers in the ditch are to be found some, who through religious cultivation, can look down, in meek superiority, upon the outwardly refined, and the book-learned.

Besides, after becoming members of this community, none will be engaged merely in bodily labor. The hours of labor for the Association will be limited by a general law, and can be curtailed at the will of the individual still more; and means will be given to all for intellectual improvement and for social intercourse, calculated to refine and expand. The hours redeemed from labor by community, will not be reapplied to the acquisition of wealth, but to the production of intellectual goods. This community aims to be rich, not in the metallic representative of wealth, but in the wealth itself, which money should represent; namely, LEISURE TO LIVE IN ALL THE FACULTIES OF THE SOUL. As a community, it will traffic with the world at large, in the products of Agricultural labor; and it will sell education to as many young persons as can be domesticated in the families, and enter into the common life with their own children. In the end, it hopes to be enabled to provide — not only all the necessaries, but all the elegances desirable for bodily and for spiritual health; books, apparatus, collections for science, works of art, means of beautiful amusement. These things are to be common to all; and thus that object, which alone gilds and refines the passion for individual accumulation, will no longer exist for desire, and whenever the Sordid passion appears, it will be seen in its naked selfishness. In its ultimate success, the community will realize all the ends which selfishness seeks, but involved in spiritual blessings, which only greatness of soul can aspire after.

And the requisitions on the individuals, it is believed, will make this the order forever. The spiritual good will always be the condition of the temporal. Every one must labor for the community in a reasonable degree, or not taste its benefits. The principles of the organization therefore, and not its probable results in future time, will determine its members. These principles are cooperation in social matters, instead of competition or balance of interests; and individual self-unfolding, in the faith that the whole soul of humanity is in each man and woman. The former is the application of the love of man; the latter of the love of God, to life. Whoever is satisfied with society, as it is; whose sense of justice is not wounded by its common action, institutions, spirit of commerce, has no business with this community; neither has any one who is willing to have other men (needing more time for intellectual cultivation than himself) give their best hours and strength to bodily labor, to secure himself immunity therefrom. And whoever does not measure what society owes to its members of cherishing and instruction, by the needs of the individuals that compose it, has no lot in this new society. Whoever is willing to receive from his fellow men that, for which he gives no equivalent, will stay away from its precincts forever.

But whoever shall surrender himself to its principles, shall find that its yoke is easy and its burden light. Everything can be said of it, in a degree, which Christ said of his kingdom, and therefore it is believed that in some measure it does embody his Idea. For its Gate of entrance is strait and narrow. It is literally a pearl *hidden in a field*. Those only who are willing to lose their life for its sake shall find it. Its voice is that which sent the young man sorrowing away. "Go sell all thy goods and give to the poor, and then come and follow me." "Seek first the kingdom of Heaven, and its righteousness, and all other things shall be added to you."

This principle, with regard to labor, lies at the root of moral and religious life; for it is not more true that "money is the root of all evil," than that *labor is the germ of all good*.

13. Amusements and Customs at Brook Farm

Lindsay Swift's light account of life at Brook Farm does not include Hawthorne's fabled first-day encounter with the manure pile, but it does give some indication of the variety and intentions of the members in this aesthetic effort at reform.

. . . Attendance at concerts and lectures away from the Farm was comparatively of infrequent occurrence; there was so much that was interesting, absorbing, and high in quality at home, that there was no particular inducement to seek diversion abroad. Whenever such excursions were taken, the motive was usually something more serious than a search for pleasure. Nothing better evinces the fine zeal of these Brook Farmers — some of them simple folk enough — than their journeying to Boston to hear good music, and then walking back a good nine miles under the stars and in the middle of the night, with an early morning's work before them. This same warm interest attached to the Associationist meetings in Boston in which Mr. Ripley usually took a leading part. Antislavery gatherings in Boston and Dedham were attended by large numbers who went in farm wagons. Only one or two of the Association were zealously committed to this cause, but it would have been impossible

Lindsay Swift, *Brook Farm* (New York, 1900), pp. 53–68.

for so humane a company to remain untouched by the call for
sympathy which was sent up all about them. One woman (Mrs.
Leach?) was so deeply imbued with antislavery feeling that she
discarded the use of the linen collar until the slave should be paid for
his work. It is not quite certain whether she confounded cotton with
flax; but her reasoning was less direct than that of Charles Lane,
who decided that linen was the only fabric which a moral man could
conscientiously wear. The use of cotton, he held, must certainly be
discouraged because it gave excuse for the employment of slave
labor; and he further argued that in our choice of wool for clothing
we rob the sheep of his natural defences. . . . When about their work
the women wore a short skirt with knickerbockers of the same
material; but when the daily tasks were ended, they attired themselves after the simpler of prevailing fashions. There was a fancy for
flowing hair and broad hats; and at the Hive dances there might be
seen wreaths woven from some of the delicate wild vines and berries
found in the woods, twined in waving locks.

It is said that the motive of economy was responsible for the
adoption, by the men, of the tunic in place of the "old-world coat."
This favorite garment was sometimes of brown holland, but often
blue, and was held in place by a black belt; and for great festivals
some of the more fortunate youths possessed black velvet tunics.
Such an unusual article of raiment excited as much dismay in the
outer world as the idiosyncrasies of other reformers, and has been
described as a compromise between the blouse of a Paris workman
and the peignoir of a possible sister. Colonel Higginson speaks of the
"picturesque little vizorless caps" worn by the young men as being
"exquisitely unfitted for horny-handed tillers of the soil." Economy
of labor may have been accountable for the unshorn face, but the
beard was certainly in high favor at Brook Farm, and a predilection
for long hair was also current. One of the residents, probably Burrill
Curtis, who had been a model for a portrait of Christ, is described by
Mrs. Kirby as a "charming feature in the landscape," while the
quality of his temper was attested by the serenity which he showed
when stoned by some boys on a pier for daring to leave his hair
unclipped in the presence of wharf rats and other good tories.

.   .   .   .   .

It is always to the credit of a reformer that he is willing to look into schemes proposed by other reformers, and Brook Farm was liberality itself toward new ideas outside its own field. The water-cure and the starving-cure both received due attention at the hands of some of the members of the household. Mrs. Kirby's account of the treatment at a cold-water cure a few miles from Brook Farm is vivid, but not alluring. Thirteen barrels of ice-cold water were yielded up daily by a natural spring, and this supply was dammed until a patient was ready for it. Then the sluices were opened and the water allowed to pour down an inclined plane and fall a distance of twenty-five feet upon the back of the shuddering victim. The sensation is said to have been that of pounding by glass balls. "Umschlag," or wet bandaging, was a treatment reserved for the following day. Strict prohibition was put on visits to the Farm in the intervals between douches, for the reason that all excitement must be avoided, in order that the cure might be efficient. The starving-cure had an ardent follower in a young Hungarian, Count G____ (possibly Gurowski though not probably), who, for a time, shared the fortunes of the Farm; but the simple menu of the community removed any pressing need for the general application of this treatment.

Of sport, in the restricted and technical sense, there is no record. People who felt doubts of the moral character of their butcher, simply because he was a butcher, could not take kindly to hunting, and probably not even to fishing. Dr. Codman says: "I do not remember ever seeing a gun on the place;" and the chances are that the woods about the Farm and the quiet waters of the Charles held undisturbed the life within them.

Columbian Phalanx

The height of Fourierist activity was between 1843 and 1850, with 13 colonies being founded in 1844. The Columbian Phalanx of Zanesville, Ohio, lasted only a year and the following account of its internal difficulties was typical of splits in other communities.

14. Account of the Columbian Phalanx

DEAR JOHN ALLEN: Again I will try to give you some idea of my whereabouts, and what I have seen. . . I have visited the Columbian Association, seven miles above Zanesville, on the Muskingum. The site of the Ohio Phalanx was beautiful, but it cannot be compared with the Columbian. Though it is winter, and the trees bare, and a slight covering of snow on the ground, yet it is the fairest spot I ever looked upon or dreamed of. There are 2700 acres, including a beautiful island formed by the branching of the Muskingum. The timber, of which there is a large quantity, is very much finer than is usual in this region. They say they could pay for the place by carrying on coopering for a few years. They have suitable timber also for boat building. There are large quantities of bituminous coal, limestone, and iron ore on the domain. They have also a beautiful stone that will polish like dark colored marble. They have a quarry

John R. Commons et al., *Documentary History of American Industrial Society* (Cleveland, 1909–11), Vol. VII, pp. 277–80.

of grindstones too — indeed it is very difficult for Northern persons to imagine the riches of this region. They have steam-boat navigation from the Ohio to the Erie Canal at Dresden. They have paid about $10,000 on the land, the cost of which was $55,000. The natural riches of the place, coal, timber, lime, iron, &c., with the crops, would enable them to pay for their place, with the greatest ease, if they had a united band upon the ground. They have one field of wheat now, containing 137 acres. They have about 150 members, though they are not all on the ground, on account of accommodations. They have thirty log buildings about twenty feet square. They have the frame of a building erected one hundred feet in length and forty in breadth — two stories high. Their land lies both sides of the Muskingum. They are, as a whole, hardly in the alphabet of social science. A few of them look to a unitary edifice — I think about fifteen of them have some idea of Fourierism. Some friends of Association went with me from Zanesville, and gave me a favorable introduction. I walked over a large part of the Domain. One good man said to me, "I wish you would tell the New England people to come out here and join us — we should certainly succeed if they would." . . The people gradually gathered together, and I preached Association and Grahamism to them in earnest. I believe I saw only one man who did not consume quantities of tobacco, and just now enormous quantities on account of a quarrel they were engaged in, which made them "very nervous." This quarrel involves the very foundations of Association, and so I shall give you a little history of it as I understood it. The founder of this Phalanx, Mr. A. B. Campbell, had become obnoxious to those members who were not imbued with any principle of association on account of his heretical notions. I can give you but little account of him, from personal observation, as I only saw him about two hours. I however laid my hand upon his head, asked him a good many questions, and heard the statements of both sides respecting him. He seems to have great intellectual power, with limited education. He was formerly a Methodist minister. He has studied what writings he could come at on Association in English, evidently with great attention. He first lectured through this region, and gathered some friends and contracted for this place. Pious people who had an idea that they could make money by uniting, advanced what of the purchasing money has been paid.

Other people of similar character wished to join, but Mr. Campbell
had made himself very obnoxious by his lectures, in which he had
criticized the religion of the day in rather the style of come-outism.
He had also spoken of civilized marriages very disrespectfully, and
moreover he worked on Sunday. One of the principal members of
the side opposed to him said to me, "Campbell is the wickedest man
in the world—he has spoken against the Bible, he has spoken against
marriage, he has worked on Sunday, he has taken in members
without property, he has said he would as lief have a black man join
as a white man." In view of all these offences, (or rather in view of
their consequence, which was that several persons who wished to
join and put in money, would not do it whilst the head of the
Association spoke against marriage, and worked on Sunday,) the
majority of the members of the Columbian Phalanx voted to expel
Mr. Campbell. The day of my arrival on the Domain, he had left.
They had no rule in their Constitution by which they could expel
him, and no definite charge against him, except that he had attended
a dance in the village, in a house which some persons thought was
not respectable. He was expelled—driven away in mid-winter without a penny, or a peck of corn, with a wife and five children. I think
he had been working for them with head or hand, about two years.
About dozen or fifteen, who have some idea of the principles of
Association, adhered to Mr. Campbell, or as they said, to the right.
The present leader who takes Mr. Campbell's place, is a sceptic, but
quite an energetic man. His impiety has not yet been objected to by
the members—probably will not be till it is found unprofitable. Day
before I left, the Fourier portion of the phalanx came to Zanesville,
and held a conversation with me respecting their difficulties and the
hopes of Association generally. There were a dozen earnest young
men who came, and Mr. Campbell was with them. I asked Mr. C.
many questions. He is a Fourierist as far as he has gone, though his
feelings are negative with regard to the sacred scriptures, I think,
owing entirely to his present excoriation by the professed believers
in the Bible. His friends, by his advice, will do all in their power to
save their place. If they cannot, they will be valuable help to some
association farther removed from chaos than this. I found that his
ideas with regard to marriage had been entirely misunderstood by

those, to whom all things are right that are according to law. The question of the relation of the sexes in Association is a momentous one; and though our friends may wish to evade or avoid it, fearing they shall be misunderstood, or that odium will attach to them if they speak out their thoughts — it must be met. . . Truly yours,

MARY S. GOVE

Wisconsin Phalanx

This account by a member of the Wisconsin phalanx places the source of their difficulties on a dispute over the question of unitary versus common dwelling houses. The unitary plan was adopted and, according to the narrator, "it induced many of the best members to leave."

15. History of the Wisconsin Phalanx by a Member

In the winter of 1843-4 there was considerable excitement in the village of Southport, Wisconsin (now Kenosha City), on the subject of Association. The subject was taken up with much feeling and interest at the village lyceum and in various public meetings. Among the advocates of Association were a few persons who determined in the spring of 1844 to make a practical experiment. For that purpose a constitution was drawn up, and a voluntary Association formed, which styled itself "The Wisconsin Phalanx." As the movement began to ripen into action, the friends fell off, and the circle narrowed down from about seventy to twenty persons. This little band was composed mostly of men with small means, sturdy constitutions, below the middle age, and full of energy; men who had been poor, and had learned early to buffet with the antagonisms of civilization; not highly cultivated in the social and intellectual faculties, but more so in the moral and industrial.

"Wisconsin Phalanx" in John H. Noyes, *History of American Socialisms* (Philadelphia, 1870), pp. 440-47.

They raised about $1,000 in money, which they sent to the land-office at Green Bay, and entered a tract of land selected by their committee, in a congressional township in the north-west corner of Fond du Lac County, a township six miles square, without a single inhabitant, and with no settlement within twenty miles, except a few scattered families about Green Lake.

With teams, stock, tents, and implements of husbandry and mechanism, they repaired to this spot in the latter part of May 1844, a distance of about one hundred and twenty-five miles from their homes, and commenced building and breaking up land, etc. They did not erect a log house, but split out of the tough burr and white oak of the "openings," shingles, clapboards, floors, frames and all the materials of a house, and soon prepared a shelter. Their families were then moved on. Late in the fall a saw-mill was built, and every thing prepared as well as could be for the winter. Their dwellings would have been unendurable at other times and under other circumstances; but at this time zeal, energy, excitement and hope kept them from complaining. Their land, which was subsequently increased to 1,800 acres, mostly at $1.25 per acre, consisted of "openings," prairie and timber, well watered, and with several small water-powers on the tract; a fertile soil, with as healthy a climate as could be found in the Western States.

It was agreed to name the new town Ceresco, and a post-office was applied for under that name, and obtained. One of the members always held the office of post-master, until the administration of General Taylor, when the office was removed about three-quarters of a mile to a rival village. In the winter of 1844-5, the Association asked the Legislature to organize their town, which was readily done under the adopted name. A few settlers had by this time moved into the town (which, owing to the large proportion of prairie, was not rapidly settled), and in the spring they held their election. Every officer chosen was a member of the society, and as they were required to elect Justices and had no need of any, they chose the three oldest men. From that time until the dissolution of the society nearly every town-office of importance was filled by its members. They had also one of their members in both Constitutional Conventions of the State, and three in the State Senate for one term of two sessions. Subsequently one of their members was a candidate for Governor, receiving more votes in his town than both of the other candidates together; but only a small vote in the State, as he was the free-soil candidate.

The Association drew up and prepared a charter or act of incorporation upon which they agreed, and applied to the Legislature for its passage; which was granted; and thus they became a body corporate and politic, known in the land as the "Wisconsin Phalanx." All the business was done in accordance with and under this charter, until the property was divided and the whole affair closed up. One clause in the charter prohibited the sale of the land. This was subsequently altered at the society's request, in an amendatory act in the session of 1849–50, for the purpose of allowing them to divide their property.

In the spring of 1845, after their organization under the charter, they had considerable accession to their numbers, and might have had greater; but were very careful about admitting new members, and erred very much in making a property qualification. About this time (1845) a question of policy arose among the members, the decision of which is supposed by many good judges to have been the principal cause of the ultimate division and dissolution; it was, whether the dwellings should be built in unitary blocks adapted to a common boarding-house, or in isolated style, adapted to the separate family and single living. It was decided by a small majority to pursue the unitary plan, and this policy was persisted in until there was a division of property. Whether this was the cause of failure or not, it induced many of the best members to leave; and although it might have been the true policy under other circumstances and for other persons, in this case it was evidently wrong, for the members were not socially developed sufficiently to maintain such close relations. Notwithstanding this, they continued to increase slowly, rejecting many more applicants than they admitted; and often rejecting the better and admitting the worse, because the worse had the property qualifications. In this way they increased to the maximum of thirty-three families. They had no pecuniary difficulties, for they kept mostly out of debt.

It was a great reading Community; often averaging as many as five or six regular newspapers to a family, and these constantly exchanging with each other. They were not religious, but mostly rather skeptical, except a few elderly orthodox persons. . . .

They were very industrious, and had many discussions and warm arguments about work, manners, progress, etc.; but still they continued to work and scold, and scold and work, with much energy, and to much effect. They raised one season ten thousand bushels of wheat, and much other grain; had about seven hundred acres under cultivation; but committed a great error in cultivating four hundred acres on the school lands adjoining their own, because it lay a little better for a large field. They had subsequently to remove their fences and leave that land, for they did not wish to buy it.

Their charter elections were annual, and were often warmly contested, and turned mainly on the question of unitary or isolated households; but they never went beyond words in their contentions.

They were all temperance men and women: no ardent spirits were kept or sold for the first four years in the township, and never on the domain, while it was held as joint-stock.

Their system of labor and pay was somewhat complicated, and never could be satisfactorily arranged. The farmers and mechanics were always jealous of each other, and could not be brought to feel near enough to work on and divide the profits at the end of the year; but as they ever hoped to get over this difficulty, they said but very little about it. In their system of labor they formed groups for each kind of work; each group, when consisting of three or more, choosing its own foreman, who kept the account of the time worked by each member, and reported weekly to a meeting of all the members, which regulated the average; and then the Secretary copied it; and at the end of the fiscal year each person drew, on his labor account, his proportion of the three-fourths of the increase and products which was allotted to labor, and on his stock shares, his proportion of the one-fourth that was divided to stock. The amount so divided was ascertained by an annual appraisal of all the property, thus ascertaining the rise or increase in value, as well as the product of labor. The dividend to capital was, however, usually considered too large and disproportionate.

The books and accounts were accurately kept by the Secretary, and most of the individual transactions passed through this form, thus leaving all accounts in the hands of a disinterested person, open to inspection at all times, and bringing about an annual settlement which avoided many difficulties incident to civilization.

The table of the Community, when kept as a public boarding-house, where the families and visitors or travelers were mostly seated, was set with plain but substantial food, much like the tables of farmers in newly settled agricultural States; but it often incurred the ridicule of loafers and epicures, who travel much and fare better with strangers than at home.

They had among their number a few men of leading intellect who always doubted the success of the experiment, and hence determined to accumulate property individually by any and every means called fair in competitive society. These would occasionally gain some important positions in the society, and representing it in part at home and abroad, caused much trouble. By some they were accounted the principal cause of the final failure.

In the summer and fall of 1849 it became evident that a dissolution and division was inevitable, and plans for doing it within themselves, without recourse to courts of law, were finally got up, and they determined to have it done by their legal advisers as other business was done. At the annual election in December 1849, the officers were elected with a view to that particular business. They had already sold much of the personal property and cancelled much of the stock. The highest amount of stock ever issued was about $33,000, and this was reduced by the sale of personal property up to January 1850, to about $23,000; soon after which the charter was amended, allowing the sale of real estate and the discontinuance of annual settlement, schools, etc.

In April 1850 they fixed on an appraisal of their lands in small lots (having some of them cut into village and farm lots), and commenced selling at public sale for stock, making the appraisal the minimum, and leaving any lands open to entry, after they had been offered publicly. During the summer of 1850 most of the lands were sold and most of the stock cancelled in this way, under an arrangement by which each stockholder should receive his proportional share of any surplus, or make up any deficiency. Most of the members bought either farming lands or village lots and became permanent inhabitants, thus continuing the society and its influences to a considerable extent. They divided about eight per cent above par on the stock.

Thus commenced, flourished and decayed this attempt at industrial Association. It never attempted to follow Fourier or any other teacher, but rather to strike out a path for itself. It failed because its leading minds became satisfied that under existing circumstances no important progress could be made, rather than from a want of faith in the ultimate practicability of Association.

Many of the members regretted the dissolution, while others who had gained property and become established in business through the reputation of the Phalanx for credit and punctuality, seemed to care very little about it. Being absorbed in the world-wide spirit of speculation, and having their minds thus occupied, they forgot the necessity for a social change, which once appeared to them so important.

Oneida

The Oneida Community, founded by John H. Noyes, combined the religious with the scientific to produce a successful and energetic response to social and sexual problems. Noyes's "Bible Communism" capitalized on the revival spirit of the day and the emerging Western fur trade to gain members and provide a solid financial base with the sale of steel traps.

From 1848 to 1868 the community practiced birth control by the use of coitus reservatus (male continence as they called it) but in 1868 it embarked on a remarkable program of planned parenthood ("stirpiculture"). In addition to its unique birth control experiment, the association practiced "complex marriage" — derided as free love by its opponents. In reality there was little that was free about the community's sex arrangements, as "matches" were conducted by an elaborate social and religious set of rules and regulations. However, there is sufficient information available to suggest that the rules served the old better than the young.

The society lasted until 1880 when, because of internal problems and some outside pressure, it gave up its unique social and sexual experiment.

John Noyes's defense of "male continence" combines the religious, the scientific, and the social in such a way as to appeal to all three audiences.

16. Male Continence

NEW YORK, July 26, 1866.

MR. _____ _____:

DEAR SIR:—Your letter addressed to the CIRCULAR, asking for information in regard to our method of controlling propagation, has been sent to me, and as it seems to come from a well-disposed person (though unknown to me) I will endeavor to give it a faithful answer—such, at least, as will be sufficient for scientific purposes.

The first question, or rather, perhaps I should say, the *previous* question in regard to Male Continence is, whether it is desirable or proper that men and women should establish intelligent voluntary control over the propagative function. Is it not better (it may be asked) to leave "nature" to take its course (subject to the general rules of legal chastity), and let children come as chance or the unknown powers may direct, without putting any restraint on sexual intercourse after it is once licensed by marriage, or on the freedom of all to take out such license? If you assent to this latter view, or have any inclination toward it, I would recommend to you the study of *Malthus on Population;* not that I think he has pointed out anything like the true *method* of voluntary control over propagation, but because he has demonstrated beyond debate the absolute *necessity* of such control in some way, unless we consent and expect that the human race, like the lower animals, shall be forever kept down to its necessary limits by the ghastly agencies of war, pestilence and famine.

For my part I have no doubt that it is perfectly proper that we should endeavor to rise above "nature" and the destiny of the brutes in this matter. There is no reason why we should not seek and hope for discovery in this direction as freely as in the development of steam power or the art of printing; and we may rationally expect that He who has promised the "good time" when vice and misery shall be abolished, will at last give us sure light on this darkest of all problems—how to subject human propagation to the control of reason.

But whether study and invention in this direction are proper or

---

John H. Noyes, *Male Continence* (Oneida, 1867), pp. 6-12.

not, they are actually at work in all quarters, reputable and disreputable. Let us see how many different ways have already been
proposed for limiting human increase.

In the first place, the practice of child-killing, either by exposure
or violence, is almost as old as the world, and as extensive as
barbarism. Even Plato recommended something of this kind, as a
waste-gate for vicious increase, in his scheme of a model republic.

Then we have the practice of abortion reduced in modern times to
a science, and almost to a distinct profession. A large part of this
business is carried on by means of medicines advertised in obscure
but intelligible terms as embryo-destroyers or preventives of conception. Every large city has its professional abortionist. Many ordinary physicians destroy embryos to order; and the skill to do this
terrible deed has even descended among the common people.

Then what a variety of artificial tricks there are for frustrating the
natural effects of the propagative act. You allude to several of these
contrivances in terms of condemnation from which I should not
dissent. The least objectionable of them, if there is any difference,
seems to be that recommended many years ago by Robert Dale
Owen, in a book entitled Moral Physiology; viz., the simple device
of withdrawing immediately before emission.

Besides all these disreputable methods, we have several more
respectable schemes for attaining the great object of limiting propagation. Malthus proposes and urges that all men, and especially the
poor, shall be taught their responsibilities in the light of science, and
so be put under inducements *not to marry*. This prudential check on
population—the discouragement of marriage—undoubtedly operates
to a considerable extent in all civilized society, and to the greatest
extent on the classes most enlightened. It seems to have been
favored by Saint Paul; (see 1st Cor. 7); and probably would not be
condemned generally by people who claim to be considerate. And
yet its advocates have to confess that it increases the danger of
licentiousness; and on the whole the teaching that is most popular, in
spite of Malthus and Paul, is that marriage, with all its liabilities, is a
moral and patriotic duty.

Finally, Shakerism, which actually prohibits marriage on religious
grounds, is only the most stringent and imposing of human contrivances for avoiding the woes of undesired propagation.

All these experimenters in the art of controlling propagation may be reduced in principle to three classes, viz.:

1. Those that seek to prevent the intercourse of the sexes, such as Malthus and the Shakers;

2. Those that seek to prevent the natural effects of the propagative act, viz.: the French inventors and Owen;

3. Those that seek to destroy the living results of the propagative act, viz.: the abortionists and child-killers.

Now it may seem to you that any new scheme of control over propagation must inevitably fall to one of these three classes; but I assure you that we have a method that does not fairly belong to any of them. I will try to show you our fourth way.

We begin by analyzing the act of sexual intercourse. It has a beginning, a middle, and an end. Its beginning and most elementary form is the simple *presence* of the male organ in the female. Then usually follows a series of reciprocal *motions*. Finally this exercise brings on a nervous action or ejaculatory *crisis* which expels the seed. Now we insist that this whole process, up to the very moment of emission, is *voluntary,* entirely under the control of the moral faculty, and *can be stopped at any point.* In other words, the *presence* and the *motions* can be continued or stopped at will, and it is only the final *crisis* of emission that is automatic or uncontrollable.

Suppose, then, that a man, in lawful intercourse with woman, choosing for good reasons not to beget a child or to disable himself, should stop at the primary stage and content himself with simple *presence* continued as long as agreeable? Would there by any harm? It cannot be injurious to refrain from voluntary excitement. Would it do no *good?* I appeal to the memory of every man who has had good sexual experience to say whether, in the whole, the sweetest and noblest period of intercourse with woman is not that *first* moment of simple presence and spiritual effusion, before the muscular exercise begins.

But we may go farther. Suppose the man chooses for good reasons, as before, to enjoy not only the simple *presence,* but also the *reciprocal motion,* and yet to stop short of the final *crisis.* Again I ask, Would there be any harm? Or would it do no good? I suppose physiologists might say, and I would acknowledge, that the excitement by motion *might* be carried so far that a voluntary suppression of the commencing crisis would be injurious. But what if a man, knowing his own power and limits, should not even *approach* the crisis, and yet be able to enjoy the presence and the motion *ad libitum?* If you say that this is impossible, I answer that I *know* it is possible — nay, that it is easy.

I will admit, however, that it may be impossible to some, while it is possible to others. Paul intimates that some cannot "contain." Men of certain temperaments and conditions are afflicted with involuntary emissions on very trivial excitement and in their sleep. But I insist that these are exceptional morbid cases that should be disciplined and improved; and that, in the normal condition, men are entirely competent to choose in sexual intercourse whether they will stop at any point in the voluntary stages of it, and so make it simply an act of communion, or go through to the involuntary stage, and make it an act of propagation.

The situation may be compared to a stream in three conditions, viz., 1, a fall; 2, a course of rapids above the fall; and 3, still water above the rapids. The skillful boatman may choose whether he will remain in the still water, or venture more or less down the rapids, or run his boat over the fall. But there is a point on the verge of the fall where he has no control over his course; and just above that there is a point where he will have to struggle with the current in a way which will give his nerves a severe trial, even though he may escape the fall. If he is willing to learn, experience will teach him the wisdom of confining his excursions to the region of easy rowing, unless he has an object in view that is worth the cost of going over the falls.

You have now our whole theory of Male Continence. It consists in analyzing sexual intercourse, recognizing in it two distinct acts, the social and the propagative, which can be separated practically, and affirming that it is best, not only with reference to prudential considerations, but for immediate pleasure, that a man should content himself with the social act, except when he intends procreation.

Let us now see if this scheme belongs to any of the three classes I mentioned. 1. It does not seek to prevent the intercourse of the sexes, but rather to prevent that which generally puts an end to such intercourse. 2. It does not seek to prevent the natural *effects* of the propagative act, but to prevent the propagative act itself, except when it is intended to be effectual. 3. Of course it does not seek to destroy the living *results* of the propagative act, but provides that impregnation and child-bearing shall be voluntary, and of course desired.

And now, to speak affirmatively, the exact thing that our theory does propose is, to take that same power of moral restraint and self-control which Paul, Malthus, the Shakers, and all considerate men use in one way or another to limit propagation, and instead of applying it, as they do, to the prevention of the intercourse of the sexes, to introduce it at another stage of the proceedings, viz., *after* the sexes have come together in social effusion, and *before* they have reached the propagative crisis; thus allowing them the most essential freedom of love, and at the same time avoiding undesired procreation and all the other evils incident to male incontinence. This is our fourth way, and we think it the better way.

The wholesale and ever ready objection to this method is that it is *unnatural, and unauthorized by the example of other animals.* I may answer in a wholesale way, that cooking, wearing clothes, living in houses, and almost everything else done by civilized man, is unnatural in the same sense, and that a close adherence to the example of the brutes would require us to forego speech and go on "all fours!" But on the other hand, if it is natural in the best sense, as I believe it is, for rational beings to forsake the example of the brutes and improve nature by invention and discovery in all directions, then truly the argument turns the other way, and we shall have to confess that until men and women find a way to elevate their sexual performances above those of the brutes, by introducing into them self-control and moral culture, they are living in *unnatural* degradation.

But I will come closer to this objection. The real meaning of it is, that Male Continence in sexual intercourse is a difficult and injurious interruption of a natural act. But every instance of self-denial is an interruption of some natural act. The man who virtuously contents himself with a look at a beautiful woman is conscious of such an interruption. The lover who stops at a kiss denies himself a natural progression. It is an easy descending grade through all the approaches of sexual love, from the first touch of respectful friendship, to the final complete amalgamation. Must there be no interruption of this natural slide? Brutes, animal or human, tolerate none. Shall their ideas of self-denial prevail? Nay, it is the glory of man to control himself, and the Kingdom of Heaven summons him to self-control in ALL THINGS. If it is noble and beautiful for the betrothed lover to respect the law of marriage in the midst of the glories of courtship, it may be even more noble and beautiful for the wedded lover to respect the laws of health and propagation in the midst of the ecstacies of sexual union. The same moral culture that ennobles the antecedents and approaches of marriage, will some time surely glorify the consummation.

Of course, you will think of many other objections and questions, and I have many answers ready for you; but I will content myself for the present with this limited presentation.

Yours respectfully,   J. H. NOYES

Icaria

The followers of Étienne Cabet, the French socialist and author of *Voyage en Icarie* (1840), started three communities between 1848 and 1858. At first they attempted to settle in Fannin County, Texas, only to find harsh weather, sickness, and bad luck. The original settlers retreated to New Orleans, where Cabet had arrived from Paris in March, 1849.

Cabet led the Icarians to a "temporary" settlement at Nauvoo, Illinois—in fact to the site of the recently abandoned Mormon colony. In 1857 a third community was established at Corning, Iowa, where the Nauvoo society functioned until 1859. In addition, a group of dissidents from Nauvoo founded a colony at Cheltenham, Missouri, in 1857; it failed in 1864.

The following account is of the Texas Icarian settlement.

17. History of Icaria

As the ship "Rome," bearing the sixty-nine pioneers, approached New Orleans on the 27th of March, its passengers heard the booming of artillery. But the salute was not in honor of their arrival. A faster ship had brought word from Paris of the Revolution of February 24th, and the French people of New Orleans were celebrating the downfall of Louis Philippe and the establishment of the Second

Albert Shaw, *Icaria: A Chapter in the History of Communism* (New York, 1884) pp. 29–37; 47–52.

Republic. If the advance guard had tarried three weeks longer in France, the subsequent history of Icaria would doubtless have been something very different from that which is recounted in the following pages. But it is for us to record what was, not what might have been.

The Revolution of 1848 was the rock on which the great Icarian school split. Part of the society advocated the recall of the advance guard, the abandonment of the emigration scheme, and the concentration of every effort for the success of the new Republic. This party hoped for the gradual transformation of France into an Icaria. But on the other hand, the party led by Cabet maintained that Icarians had nothing to hope from a government controlled by Lamartine, Ledru-Rollin, and others hostile to the Communistic cause. In reality, Louis Blanc, Blanqui, Cabet, and the extremists were now, as in 1830, the men who had precipitated the revolution; but, as before, they were unable to control its results. Louis Blanc was the only one of their number who obtained a leading place in the new government, and in accordance with his views a series of reforms were at once instituted, almost precisely in the line of those contained in Cabet's "transitional constitution," described in the "Voyage." The "right to labor" was proclaimed by law, and in a few weeks, more than a hundred thousand men were employed in national workshops. Taxes on salt, and other indirect taxes on the necessaries of life were removed, and direct taxes were almost doubled. The interests of the laboring man were solicitously, ostentatiously regarded in the legislation of the Republic. The length of a day's labor was fixed by law. Wages were made matter of legislation. But the triumph of socialism was brief, the workshops proved a dismal failure, and the reform legislation survived only a few weeks. The whole situation, however, placed Cabet in a painful dilemma. He decided that he could not wisely abandon the colonization, and the hitherto devoted and harmonious body of Icarians was fatally severed.

On the 3d of June the second advance guard left France, but it was not the corps of 1,000 or 1,500 men that had been promised. It was a resolute band of only nineteen!

Here let us turn to follow the fortunes of the sixty-nine pioneers. On learning in New Orleans that the Republic had been proclaimed in France, the question of immediate return was agitated. This view did not prevail, although three or four men left the party determined to go back. It was ascertained that in order to reach the lands of the Peters Company they must go to Shreveport, Louisiana, on the Red River, by steamboat, and advance thence to their destination by teams. The *Populaire* had stated that the land acquired from Peters was washed by the Red River and would be readily accessible by boat; but òn arriving at Shreveport the advance guard discovered a very momentous geographical discrepancy. Icaria was more than two hundred and fifty miles distant (some thirty miles distant from the spot where the city of Dallas now flourishes), and must be reached by a march across a wellnigh trackless wilderness of plains and hills, prairies and forests, undrained swamps and unbridged streams, swollen by the spring rains. Like most emigrants, these pilgrims were encumbered with much unnecessary luggage, and provided with too little ready money. They spent several days in Shreveport trying in vain to procure wagons and teams for the conveyance of their goods to Sulphur Prairie. (Sulphur Prairie, be it said, was a farm about a hundred miles from Shreveport, which Sully, Cabet's commissioner, had bought as an Icarian rendezvous and base of operations; and at this time Sully himself was lying sick at Sulphur Prairie.) Finally a portion of the guard started, with two or three ox-teams and one wagon: The others remained behind until they had completed a large temporary shed on the edge of the village, in which shed they stored their troublesome and bulky belongings. A most graphic account of the weary trudge on foot from Shreveport to Sulphur Prairie and thence to Icaria was written by Levi de Rheims on the 2d of June, a very few days after his arrival on the scene of the "new terrestrial paradise." This letter, written to relatives and friends in France, found its way into print, and a copy of it is among my materials for this sketch. From the arrival at New Orleans to the arrival at Icaria, almost two months had elapsed. Strangers in a strange land, unable to speak English, ignorant of almost every thing which a pioneer should know, their hardships were only exceeded by their fortitude and good cheer. Sickness by the way, the breaking down of their one wagon, the wading of dangerous streams, the insufficient supply of food, sleeping on the damp ground, — the whole situation can hardly be realized by one who has not experienced something of life in a wilderness.

At Sulphur Prairie they found a new cause of anxiety and haste.

They had been assured by Cabet and by the *Populaire* that a million acres of land had already been acquired. Here also, as in the case of the geographical situation, they found a painful discrepancy. The acquisition was discovered to be not absolute, but on condition of actual colonization. Each man could secure and hold a half-section (320 acres) by building a house upon it and living therein. This would give free possession. But this offer held good only until July 1st. After that date, land would have to be purchased at one dollar an acre. When July 1st arrived, it was found that their utmost efforts had availed to build thirty-two very small log-cabins. They were, therefore, in possession, not of 1,000,000 acres, but of 10,240. As it was a journey of more than three months from Paris to Icaria, emigrants leaving France later than the month of March could not possibly have arrived in time to secure land under the contract with Peters.

But it remains to relate another sad discrepancy. The thirty-two half-sections were not contiguous! The State of Texas had granted to the Peters Company each alternate section (square mile, 640 acres) of a certain tract of land, on condition that the company should secure immigration. The company had in turn granted the Icarians the privilege of acquiring by actual residence the half of each of its sections, to the extent of a million acres. Cabet's million acres would therefore have been checkered over a territory of four millions, and the 10,240 acres were scattered through two townships. . . .

It needs no argument to show that a colony intending to live grouped in a village, with a unitary *cuisine* and dining-hall and a cooperative system of agriculture and industry, must have its land in a compact body. The possibility of buying the alternate half-sections from Mr. Peters and the alternate sections from the State of Texas was entirely too remote and uncertain to have been relied upon. In spite of all this disheartening outlook, the pioneers kept pretty good spirits, and set resolutely to work to establish a central headquarters, in anticipation of the large arrivals expected. A log-house fifteen feet wide by twenty-five long was achieved, and three or four long covered sheds. The summer was far advanced, but it was obviously necessary to put in a crop. A plow had been purchased, and they set about "breaking" prairie. But alas! they knew not how. In turning the matted virgin sod of the prairie for the first time, the Western farmer never sinks his plow-share deeper than two or three inches; but these young French tailors and shoemakers knew nothing about Western farming, and they drove the plow in clear to the beam. It was what is known in Western parlance as a large "breaking plow," and they fastened twenty oxen to it. They broke their plow very promptly, but they never "broke" any Texas prairie. For by this time the middle of July was past, and man after man succumbed to an intermittent malarial fever, till there was not a well person in the camp. The unaccustomed heat, their arduous and imprudent labors, and their unacclimated condition had subjected them to a terrible scourge. Their physician became sick, then hopelessly insane. Four men soon died of the fever. Another was killed by lightning. Those least sick prepared food and cared for their more helpless comrades.

August was passing away. It was now too late to think of putting in a crop, even if they had been able to do the work. It took letters several months to reach France, and they knew that before word could be received from Texas their own wives and families, as well as many additional Icarians, would have embarked for America. To prepare either the settlement on the Peters lands or the camp at Sulphur Prairie for the winter-quarters of a large body of immigrants was now seen to be practically impossible. In June, the pioneers had been cheerful, and had written home glowing, enthusiastic accounts of the beauty and evident richness of the vast prairies, with their fine streams bordered with heavy timber fringes. But a wild southwestern prairie in the flowery months of May and June seems a much more inviting and hospitable place than under the withering sun and scorching winds of August. The fever had dispirited the Icarians, and the country had become loathsome to them. They resolved to abandon it. Indeed, to have done otherwise would have been mistaken heroism.

Amana

When Charles Nordhoff visited the Amana colonies in 1874 he found a prosperous, large (1,450 members on 25,000 acres), and well-established community. Under the leadership of Christian Metz, these German pietists had come to the United States in 1842 and had settled near Buffalo, New York. In 1855 they sold their 8,000 acres in New York and moved to Iowa, where they continued to farm.

In 1932 the community became a corporation. It now operates over 30 enterprises, including a winery and a woolens factory.

18. Visit in 1874

"The name we took out of the Bible," said one of the officers of the society to me. They put the accent on the first syllable. The name occurs in the Song of Solomon, the fourth chapter and eighth verse: "Come with me from Lebanon, my spouse, with me from Lebanon: look from the top of Amana, from the top of Shenir and Hermon, from the lions' dens, from the mountains of the leopards."

Amana in Iowa, however, is not a mountain, but an extensive plain, upon which they have built seven villages, conveniently placed so as to command the cultivated land, and to form an irregular circle within their possessions. In these villages all the people live, and they are thus divided:

Charles Nordhoff, *The Communistic Societies of the United States* (New York: Harper and Brothers, 1875), pp. 31–43.

Name.	Population.	Business.
Amana	450	Woolen-mill, saw and grist mill, and farming.
East Amana	125	Farming.
Middle Amana	350	Woolen-mill and farming.
Amana near the Hill	125	Farming, saw-mill, and tannery.
West Amana	150	Grist-mill and farming.
South Amana	150	Saw-mill and farming.
Homestead	135	Railroad station, a saw-mill, farming, and general depot.

The villages lie about a mile and a half apart, and each has a store at which the neighboring farmers trade, and a tavern or inn for the accommodation of the general public. Each village has also its shoe-makers', carpenters', tailors', and other shops, for they aim to produce and make, as far as possible, all that they use. In Middle Amana there is a printing-office, where their books are made.

The villages consist usually of one straggling street, outside of which lie the barns, and the mills, factories, and work-shops. The houses are well built, of brick, stone, or wood, very plain; each with a sufficient garden, but mostly standing immediately on the street. They use no paint, believing that the wood lasts as well without. There is usually a narrow sidewalk of boards or brick; and the school-house and church are notable buildings only because of their greater size. Like the Quakers, they abhor "steeple-houses;" and their church architecture is of the plainest. The barns and other farm buildings are roomy and convenient. On the boundaries of a village are usually a few houses inhabited by hired laborers.

Each family has a house for itself; though when a young couple marry, they commonly go to live with the parents of one or the other for some years.

As you walk through a village, you notice that at irregular intervals are houses somewhat larger than the rest. These are either cook-houses or prayer-houses. The people eat in common, but for convenience' sake they are divided, so that a certain number eat together. For Amana, which has 450 people, there are fifteen such cooking and eating houses. In these the young women are employed to work under the supervision of matrons; and hither when the bell rings come those who are appointed to eat at each — the sexes sitting at separate tables, and the children also by themselves.

"Why do you separate men from women at table?" I asked. "To prevent silly conversation and trifling conduct," was the answer.

Food is distributed to the houses according to the number of persons dining in each. Meal and milk are brought to the doors; and each cooking-house is required to make its own butter and cheese. For those whom illness or the care of small children keeps at home, the food is placed in neat baskets; and it was a curious sight to see, when the dinner-bell rang, a number of women walking rapidly about the streets with these baskets, each nicely packed with food.

When the bell ceases ringing and all are assembled, they stand up in their places in silence for half a minute, then one says grace, and when he ends, all say, "God bless and keep us safely," and then sit down. There is but little conversation at table; the meal is eaten rapidly, but with decorum; and at its close, all stand up again, some one gives thanks, and thereupon they file out with quiet order and precision.

They live well, after the hearty German fashion, and bake excellent bread. The table is clean, but it has no cloth. The dishes are coarse but neat; and the houses, while well built, and possessing all that is absolutely essential to comfort according to the German peasants' idea, have not always carpets, and have often a bed in what New-Englanders would call the parlor; and in general are for use and not ornament.

They breakfast between six and half-past six, according to the season, have supper between six and seven, and dinner at half-past eleven. They have besides an afternoon lunch of bread and butter and coffee, and in summer a forenoon lunch of bread, to which they add beer or wine, both home-made.

They do not forbid tobacco.

Each business has its foreman; and these leaders in each village meet together every evening, to concert and arrange the labors of the following day. Thus if any department needs for an emergency an extra force, it is known, and the proper persons are warned. The trustees select the temporal foremen, and give to each from time to time his proper charge, appointing him also his helpers. Thus a member showed me his "ticket," by which he was appointed to the care of the cows, with the names of those who were to assist him. In the summer, and when the work requires it, a large force is turned into the fields; and the women labor with the men in the harvest. The workmen in the factories are, of course, not often changed.

The children are kept at school between the ages of six and thirteen; the sexes do not sit in separate rooms. The school opens at seven o'clock, and the children study and recite until half-past nine. From that hour until eleven, when they are dismissed for dinner, they knit gloves, wristlets, or stockings. At one o'clock school re-opens, and they once more attend to lessons until three, from which hour till half-past four they knit again. The teachers are men, but they are relieved by women when the labor-school begins. Boys as well as girls are required to knit. One of the teachers said to me that this work kept them quiet, gave them habits of industry, and kept them off the streets and from rude plays.

They instruct the children in musical notation, but do not allow musical instruments. They give only the most elementary in-struction, the "three Rs," but give also constant drill in the Bible and in the Catechism. "Why should we let our youth study? We need no lawyers or preachers; we have already three doctors. What they need is to live holy lives, to learn God's commandments out of the Bible, to learn submission to his will, and to love him."

The dress of the people is plain. The men wear in the winter a vest which buttons close up to the throat, coat and trousers being of the common cut.

The women and young girls wear dingy colored stuffs, mostly of the society's own make, cut in the plainest style, and often short gowns, in the German peasant way. All, even to the very small girls, wear their hair in a kind of black cowl or cap, which covers only the back of the head, and is tied under the chin by a black ribbon. Also all, young as well as old, wear a small dark-colored shawl or hand-kerchief over the shoulders, and pinned very plainly across the breast. This peculiar uniform adroitly conceals the marks of sex, and gives a singularly monotonous appearance to the women.

The sex, I believe, is not highly esteemed by these people, who think it dangerous to the Christian's peace of mind. One of their most esteemed writers advises men to "fly from intercourse with women, as a very highly dangerous magnet and magical fire." Their women work hard and dress soberly; all ornaments are forbidden. To wear the hair loose is prohibited. Great care is used to keep the sexes apart. In their evening and other meetings, women not only sit apart from men, but they leave the room before the men break ranks. Boys are allowed to play only with boys, and girls with girls. There are no places or occasions for evening amusements, where the sexes might meet. On Sunday afternoons the boys are permitted to walk in the fields; and so are the girls, but these must go in another direction. "Perhaps they meet in the course of the walk," said a member to me, "but it is not allowed." At meals and in their labors they are also separated. With all this care to hide the charms of the young women, to make them, as far as dress can do so, look old and ugly, and to keep the young men away from them, love, courtship, and marriage go on at Amana as elsewhere in the world. The young man "falls in love," and finds ways to make his passion known to its object; he no doubt enjoys all the delights of courtship, intensified by the difficulties which his prudent brethren put in his way; and he marries the object of his affection, in spite of her black hood and her sad-colored little shawl, whenever he has reached the age of twenty-four.

For before that age he may not marry, even if his parents consent. This is a merely prudential rule. "They have few cares in life, and would marry too early for their own good—food and lodging being secured them—if there were not a rule upon the subject;" so said one of their wise men to me. Therefore, no matter how early the young people agree to marry, the wedding is deferred until the man reaches the proper age.

And when at last the wedding-day comes, it is treated with a degree of solemnity which is calculated to make it a day of terror rather than of unmitigated delight. The parents of the bride and groom meet, with two or three of the elders, at the house of the bride's father. Here, after singing and prayer, that chapter of Paul's writings is read wherein, with great plainness of speech, he describes to the Ephesians and the Christian world in general the duties of husband and wife. On this chapter the elders comment "with great thoroughness" to the young people, and "for a long time," as I was told; and after this lecture, and more singing and prayer, there is a modest supper, whereupon all retire quietly to their homes.

The strictly pious hold that marriages should be made only by consent of God, signified through the "inspired instrument."

While the married state has thus the countenance and sanction of the society and its elders, matrimony is not regarded as a meritorious act. It has in it, they say, a certain large degree of worldliness; it is not calculated to make them more, but rather less spiritually minded—so think they at Amana—and accordingly the religious standing of the young couple suffers and is lowered. In the Amana church there are three "classes," orders or grades, the highest consisting of those members who have manifested in their lives the greatest spirituality and piety. Now, if the new-married couple should have belonged for years to this highest class, their wedding would put them down into the lowest, or the "children's order," for a year or two; until they had won their slow way back by deepening piety.

The civil or temporal government of the Amana communists consists of thirteen trustees, chosen annually by the male members of the society. The president of the society is chosen by the trustees.

This body manages the finances, and carries on the temporalities generally, but it acts only with the unanimous consent of its members. The trustees live in different villages, but exercise no special authority, as I understand, as individuals. The foremen and elders in each village carry on the work and keep the accounts. Each village keeps its own books and manages its own affairs; but all accounts are finally sent to the head-quarters at Amana, where they are inspected, and the balance of profit or loss is discovered. It is supposed that the labor of each village produces a profit; but whether it does or not makes no difference in the supplies of the people, who receive every thing alike, as all property is held in common. All accounts are balanced once a year, and thus the productiveness of every industry is ascertained.

The elders are a numerous body, not necessarily old men, but presumably men of deep piety and spirituality. They are named or appointed by inspiration, and preside at religious assemblies.

In every village four or five of the older and more experienced elders meet each morning to advise together on business. This council acts, as I understand, upon reports of those younger elders who are foremen and have charge of different affairs. These in turn meet for a few minutes every evening, and arrange for the next day's work.

Women are never members of these councils, nor do they hold, as far as I could discover, any temporal or spiritual authority, with the single exception of their present spiritual head, who is a woman of eighty years. Moreover, if a young man should marry out of the society, and his wife should desire to become a member, the husband is expelled for a year—at the end of which time both may make application to come in, if they wish.

They have contrived a very simple and ingenious plan for supplying their members with clothing and other articles aside from food. To each adult male an annual allowance is made of from forty to one hundred dollars, according as his position and labor necessitates more or less clothing. For each adult female the allowance is from twenty-five to thirty dollars, and from five to ten dollars for each child.

All that they need is kept in store in each village, and is sold to the members at cost and expenses. When any one requires an article of clothing, he goes to the store and selects the cloth, for which he is charged in a book he brings with him; he then goes to the tailor, who makes the garment, and charges him on the book an established price. If he needs shoes, or a hat, or tobacco, or a watch, every thing is in the same way charged. As I sat in one of the shops, I noticed women coming in to make purchases, often bringing children with them, and each had her little book in which due entry was made. "Whatever we do not use, is so much saved against next year; or we may give it away if we like," one explained to me; and added that during the war, when the society contributed between eighteen and twenty thousand dollars to various benevolent purposes, much of this was given by individual members out of the savings on their year's account.

Almost every man has a watch, but they keep a strict rule over vanities of apparel, and do not allow the young girls to buy or wear ear-rings or breastpins.

The young and unmarried people, if they have no parents, are divided around among the families.

They have not many labor-saving contrivances; though of course the eating in common is both economical and labor-saving. There is in each village a general wash-house, where the clothing of the unmarried people is washed, but each family does its own washing.

They have no libraries; and most of their reading is in the Bible, and in their own "inspired" records, which, as I shall show further on, are quite voluminous. A few newspapers are taken, and each calling among them receives the journal which treats of its own specialty. In general they aim to withdraw themselves as much as possible from the world, and take little interest in public affairs. During the war they voted; "but we do not now, for we do not like the turn politics have taken"—which seemed to me a curious reason for refusing to vote.

Their members came originally from many parts of Germany and Switzerland; they have also a few "Pennsylvania Dutch." They have much trouble with applicants who desire to join the society; and receive, the secretary told me, sometimes dozens of letters in a month from persons of whom they know nothing; and not a few of whom, it seems, write, not to ask permission to join, but to say that they are coming on at once. There have been cases where a man wrote to say that he had sold all his possessions, and was then on the way, with his family, to join the association. As they claim to be not an industrial, but a religious community, they receive new members with great care, and only after thorough investigation of motives and religious faith; and these random applications are very annoying to them. Most of their new members they receive from Germany, accepting them after proper correspondence, and under the instructions of "inspiration." Where they believe them worthy they do not inquire about their means; and a fund is annually set apart by the trustees to pay the passage of poor families whom they have determined to take in.

Usually a neophyte enters on probation for two years, signing an obligation to labor faithfully, to conduct himself according to the society's regulations, and to demand no wages. If at the close of his probation he appears to be a proper person, he is admitted to full membership; and if he has property, he is then expected to put this into the common stock; signing also the constitution, which provides that on leaving he shall have his contribution returned, but without interest.

There are cases, however, where a new-comer is at once admitted to full membership. This is where "inspiration" directs such breach of the general rule, on the ground that the applicant is already a fit person. . . .

They lose very few of their young people. Some who leave them return after a few years in the world. Plain and dull as the life is, it appears to satisfy the youth they train up; and no doubt it has its rewards in its regularity, peacefulness, security against want, and freedom from dependence on a master.

It struck me as odd that in cases of illness they use chiefly homeopathic treatment. The people live to a hale old age. They had among the members, in March, 1874, a woman aged ninety-seven, and a number of persons over eighty.

They are non-resistants; but during the late war paid for substitutes in the army. "But we did wrongly there," said one to me; "it is not right to take part in wars even in this way."

To sum up: the people of Amana appeared to me a remarkably quiet, industrious, and contented population; honest, of good repute among their neighbors, very kindly, and with religion so thoroughly and largely made a part of their lives that they may be called a religious people.

From Communism to Socialism

The post-Civil War period saw a marked decline in both the number of communities started and their social significance. The communitarian ideal was rendered obsolete by the industrial revolution as labor union and socialist political activity captured much of the community spirit. There were some groups that served as transitions into the new age—such as Alcander Longley's Altruist community in St. Louis and those associations, like Oneida and Amana, with a religious impulse that carried them longer than the secular societies.

Whereas men had called themselves communists in the 1840's and 50's, they were now known as "socialists" searching for new models in the machine age. For example, the Oneida community began its history devoted to "Bible Communism," only to end it with the publication of a journal titled *The American Socialist.* William Hinds, a member of Oneida and author of *American Communities,* wrote in 1878 that there are

numerous Cooperative stores and Cooperative manufacturing companies in the Northern States, and even large Orders, like the Granges and the Sovereigns of Industry, and a Socialist Labor Party, that might be mentioned in this connection as additional evidences that a tidal wave of Socialism—using the term in its broadest sense—is bearing onward toward conditions more accordant with its ultimate destiny.

Hinds had joined Oneida as a young man, and when he wrote about the tidal wave of socialism, Oneida was two years away from dissolution. However, a good utopian must interpret history and historical circumstances progressively if he is to remain sane. For even if the older religious and secular experiments of the forties and fifties had begun to wane, there was additional evidence, at least to men like Hinds, that the new order was imminent.

Some sought relief in cooperative homes or joint-stock ventures, while others took the higher road of spiritualism in order to transcend social and economic reality. All of these schemes had been tried before the Civil War, but the utopian mind is not interested in past failures — only future successes. Needless to say, they ran into the same problems of leadership, internal dissension, and fading hopes as had their predecessors.

Brotherhood of the New Life

The move westward was inevitable for the utopian communities, and California proved a hospitable site for many of the late 19th-century groups. There were located religious groups like Fountain Grove, Point Loma, Pisgah Grande, and Temple Grove, and secular societies like Kaweah, Altruria, Joyful, Llano, and Army of Industry. Most of the California groups followed a socialistic pattern in which all the means of production were held in common. In some cases individuals maintained holdings in the outside world, and in the case of the Theosophists at Point Loma individual home ownership was allowed within the community. Again the range of philosophies, interests, and capacities was wide, reflecting the numerous roots of the impulse to form a community.

One of the deepest roots in the communitarian tradition is the spiritualist one; it emphasizes a fellowship of souls that both binds an individual to his fellow man and enables him to transcend the material world. The Brotherhood of the New Life under the guidance of Thomas Lake Harris was the first of the California spiritualist groups. Harris was a Universalist minister who became a disciple of the famous spiritualist Andrew Jackson Davis in the 1840's. From spiritualism he moved into Swedenborgianism, then into his own mixture of the two.

Robert Hine has characterized the Brotherhood of the New Life as the "product of ecclesiastical revolt, Christianity and spiritualism and Swedenborgianism mixed in the mind of

Harris with later additions of Oriental mysticism and late nineteenth century anti-monopoly socialism." Harris ruled the celibate community in patriarchal fashion, listening for spiritual inspiration as guidance.

A trip to England in the early sixties resulted in the conversion of Lady Oliphant and her son Laurence. With financial aid from the Oliphants, Harris was able to move from his Amenia, New York, community to Brocton on Lake Erie.

In 1875 he moved, with a small group of followers, to Santa Rosa, California, where he maintained a colony until 1892, when stories about sexual irregularities forced Harris to leave Santa Rosa.

19. Letter of Thomas Lake Harris

FOUNTAIN GROVE, SANTA ROSA, CAL., Aug. 22, 1877.
W. A. HINDS, *Dear Sir:—*

The life, system and action of the Society which I represent are so far removed from the lines of the usual thought, that I fear I shall hardly be able to answer your friendly inquiries with the fullness you desire. Personally, I am not a Communist. I find it impossible to maintain the ordinary relations; much more to unite in close association, communistically, with even my nearest friends. My home is practically an hermitage: the evolution of my faculties has led me into strict natural celibacy. Whatever material property I possess is considered by me as fully my own; yet not my own, being held, like all other gifts, as a trust from God, for his service in the race. Both physically and morally I find it impossible to exist under other conditions.

While thus self-contained, reserved and isolated, I find myself enzoned by a large circle of men and women, in Europe and Asia, as well as in this country, who have been driven to me by a potent attraction, in the course of my labors, but without any conscious

William Hinds, *American Communities* (Oneida, 1878), pp. 142–48.

endeavor of my own. My life is devoted to their service, and I feel honored in their inexpressible love and devotion. They constitute the Society known as the "Brotherhood of the New Life." Of their numbers, wealth, or potential force, I do not feel at liberty to speak.

My people, with few exceptions, reside in isolated families, and esteem it fortunate that thus far they have generally escaped the intrusive curiosity of the civilizees. This is a kingdom that does not come with observation: it employs no verbal preachers: it practices no ecclesiastical rites: it seeks no mere natural proselytes: its voice is not heard in the street. Yet it affects no mystery, and those who desire to know of it for "the good of life" find no difficulty in attaining to what they seek. It grows simply by its power of organic diffusion and assimilation. We believe it to be a germ of the Kingdom of Heaven, dropped from upper space and implanted in the bosom of the earthly humanity: — in fine, the seed of a new order; the initial point for a loftier and sweeter evolution of man.

Two only of our Families, so far as I am aware, have fallen under the eye of correspondents of the press; that in the town of Portland, Chautauqua Co., N.Y., and this, my private residence, in California. These are practically one. In both of them the social order may perhaps be termed patriarchal, there being no community of possessions. I may quote from the old dramatist, and say: "A poor house, sir, but mine own." I hope I shall not trespass on the modest privacy of my guests and kinsmen, if I add that, under no stress of compulsion, but in the evolution of character, they have become, in the natural sense, celibate as I am: some entering from a state of monogamic marriage, but others virginal from the first.

Of the other Families in the Society, I may say that they are in different stages of advancement, from a starting-point of accepted altruism; that they begin from germs of individual households, with no break in the continuity of relations; the new growth forming in the old wood of the tree; the internal first changing, and then, by evolution, "that which is without" becoming "as that which is within." All growths are first invisible. After seventeen years of life, unity and struggle, the Brotherhood begins to declare its presence and purpose. Notices that you may have seen of it, like the sensational article in the *New York Sun,* published some years since, have been unauthorized accounts, and such facts as served to give them color and credence were obtained under the express understanding that they should be held in honorable confidence. In evolving a new spiritual experience, through a new social experience, we have sought to avoid publicity. It is time enough to describe a tree when it begins to ripen its fruit.

The Family at

SALEM-ON-ERIE,

which these press notices have brought into unwelcome observation, under the *pseudonym* of the "Brocton Community," was founded in the town of Amenia, Dutchess Co., N.Y., in the spring of 1861. It removed to its present locality in, I think, 1867. In Dr. Taylor's "History of Portland," which I mail to your address, you will find a brief *résumé* of its material and industrial affairs and of its labors at the date of publication, 1873. During the ensuing year the Family began to contract its affairs. Its industries are now confined to the orchard, vineyard and farm. Never so united, never so effective in unity, it maintains a waiting attitude.

This Family passed, years ago, through the communistic phase, in which, however, I did not take part, though esteeming it a phase in evolution and serving it financially. As a means of education it was useful, but those engaged in it found that, in the long run, it was neither promotive of their happiness, nor evolutionary in the direction of their ruling tendencies.

Without dissension or disunion, its members then passed into a phase of modified Socialism, each series constituting a family partnership, and found that this mode of combined action developed a large force of individual character, as well as a more strict business habit and aptitude. Here the ledger showed a favorable balance, but the spirit was not fully satisfied.

Meantime I organized my own affairs, amidst my friends, and employed all who did not fit or find place elsewhere, treating them as sons, but insisting on paying weekly wages. After a time they found it incompatible with their forming affections to receive money-pay.

I then entertained them as guests, brethren and children in their father's house; and this satisfied. They labor for me, and I for them: their services, recreations and expenses are regulated among themselves. I put limits on their labors, but not on their recreations or expenses. There is no espionage: honor rules: love is supreme.

Gradually the family partnerships have ceased, without a struggle, and all have entered into this order.

In serving me these tender hearts believe that they are also serving God, working for a kingdom of universal righteousness. They do not think that I possess any thing, except as representatively; nor that I rule in them, except as aiding to lift and direct them into a larger freedom, wisdom and purity. I consider the Family at Salem-on-Erie and that at Fountain Grove as one: the germ of a solar family in the midst of a planetary family system.

I find no difficulty in the solution of the painful and perplexing problem of the sexes. Monogamists who enter into union with me rise, by changes of life, into a desire for the death of natural sexuality. Those whose lives have been less strict first, perhaps, may pass through the monogamic relation, though not always; but the end is the same. Others, who have lived singly, holding the fierce passion in restraint, find themselves gliding out of the passional tempest into a bodily state of serenity and repose. Still I do not believe that sexlessness characterizes man in his higher and final evolution.

Among my people, as they enter into the peculiar evolution that constitutes the new life, two things decrease: the propagation of the species and physical death. In the large patriarchal Family that I have described but one death has occurred since its formation in 1861, and this under circumstances and with results which demonstrated to us that the dear and honored subject of the visitation was simply taken from his more visible place to serve as an intermediate for higher services. One young pair in our borders have had three children, I am sorry to say; but with this exception the births in seventeen years have been but two, and of these the younger is almost a young man. We think that generation must cease till the sons and daughters of God are prepared for the higher generation, by evolution into structural, bisexual completeness, above the plane of sin, of disease, or of natural mortality.

I have considered my Family, since 1861, merely as a school: its methods educationary, and its form only tentative. My aim, *per se,* has been neither to organize close nor far-apart association, but to prepare myself and the inmates of my house for *a new era of human evolution,* which we have considered to be at hand, and which in individual cases we think has now begun. We think that by the survival of the fittest, the most plastic, the most complex organisms, men of a new spirit wrought bodily into new structures, the race will take a new departure; that we approach a new beginning of human days and generations.

I may add here that our views are not the result of mere scriptural study, nor based on textual interpretations, and that we have no especial sympathy that unites us to one school of religionists more than to another. If we find one vein of knowledge, or possibly correct surmise, in Swedenborg, we find other veins in Spinoza, or Böehme, or Comte. Using the term in its metaphysical sense, we aim not to be partialists but universalists of inquiry and knowledge. We consider all Scriptures as literature; we hold that experience is the measure and method of revelation; and that, for the ripening of experience, man should be both individualized and insociated. Believers in the Divine Immanence, we hold by the "True Light, that lighteth every man who cometh into the world;" but we further conclude that the Creative Logos, "God manifested in the flesh," is not male merely, or female merely, but the two-in-one. The doctrine of the Divine-human Two-in-One, in whose individual and social likeness, in whose spiritual and physical likeness, we seek to be re-born, is the pivot of our faith and the directive force of our life. The ages wait for the manifestation of the sons of God. Thus we are adventists, not in a sectarian sense, but in the sense of a divine involution, and thence of a new degree in human evolution. Our faith teaches us love for all men, however inverted, arrested, or infirm, as our dear brethren. Our sympathies are especially toward those who have devoted themselves, in a practical sense, to the substitution of "altruism" for egoism, of mutuality for competition, in social life.

With these views you will readily perceive why the Brotherhood of the New-Life has both sought to maintain a modest privacy, and to keep aloof from the prevalent discussions of social amelioration and reform.

With kind regards, believe me

Faithfully yours,   T. L. HARRIS

Altruria

The Altruria colony had a short but happy history as its founders—a group of Christian Socialists led by a Unitarian minister from Berkeley—spend a year (1894–95) trying to establish an economic base on 185 acres near Santa Rosa, California. Imbued with the idealism of a George Herron and supported by other Altrurist societies throughout the state, they farmed, ran a hotel, and published the *Altrurian*. All, however, to little avail, as they failed to turn a profit and broke up in less than a year.

Morrison Swift, who visited the Altrurists a number of times, indicates their basic humanity and social concerns within a Christian Socialist framework of cooperation.

20. Altruria in California

Fifty miles north of San Francisco, in the Santa Rosa valley, the soil is rich and the climate perfect for a co-operative experiment. The founders chose two hundred acres of land beautifully encircled by hills, with plentiful water for irrigation and power, and a vein of coal running beneath. The ranchers of the surrounding country are intelligent and kindly and not averse to new ideas and methods.

This colony was to be a refuge for those strained and tired by

Morrison Swift, "Altruria in California," *Overland Monthly*, Vol. XXIX (June, 1897), pp. 643–45.

competition or defeated in the struggle. The terms of entrance were therefore light, fifty dollars and a moral character being sufficient passport to membership. The Association proposed "to buy, sell, and hold land, erect buildings, institute agricultural, mechanical, and manufacturing industries, establish schools, libraries, and institutions of art, found co-operative colonies," and otherwise labor to illustrate and extend the cooperative method. The colonists hoped that the fraternal spirit of industry would be contagious, that colony after colony would spring up, until not only the surplus laborers of society were absorbed but people of means had joined and transferred their ranches and manufactories to the commune. By the success of joint friendly association in production it was hoped to wean all society from egotism and individualism to a broad and practical altruism.

The colony did not do this, but it performed much else. The first year was purely experimental, finding out the right basis. The discovery was made that a carefully selected group of persons would be necessary to give form and direction to the undertaking, and a re-organization was effected, reducing the membership from fifty-six to twenty-one. With the small capital and the small amount of immediately cultivable land the larger number could not live. A probationary residence of six months was required of each applicant for admission. The members found that the colony method of co-operation had not reached a stage that would ensure success to any combination of persons formed at random, who might be drawn to the community plan of life. After reorganizing they sought to complete such an experiment, to use it to teach the importance of national co-operation, or national ownership of industries, as well as of community co-operation.

Altruria was a picturesque and attractive demonstration of society without classes. It had no servant order and no superior caste of idlers, and the gratitude one felt at escaping from these trials grew with each day's residence. The tasks were divided among all the members as the preference of each decided, and through the pleasant association of intelligent workers the ordinary irksomeness and monotony of labor disappeared. The office of "laundry-lady" was especially sought after on account of the prevailing fun in the laundry department. All ate in a common dining room and the members, particularly the younger ones, took turns in waiting upon the tables.

The food was chiefly obtained from the vegetable garden of the colony, and was cooked in a manner that made the outsider envious and converted the most selfish to altruism.

Each member presented his entire property to the community and signed a contract to take away only such as the association should allow him, if he saw fit at any time thereafter to withdraw. Some of the members possessed no wealth to contribute, while others brought in several thousand dollars each.

The labor of the members was divided between perfecting the material foundations of the institution and publishing a paper. The best outdoor work centered in the land, from which several wagon loads of produce were sold weekly at Santa Rosa, beyond the consumption of the community. A large building, for the colony dwelling and as a hotel for guests, was erected but not wholly finished. Its spacious parlors were intended to provide a place for public meetings and lectures, of which a number were given. This phase of association life is to be studied in contrast with the intellectual isolation of average families. One evening a week the Altrurians met to hear an original paper from one of their number, and each Sunday morning services were held, consisting of music and an address from some member, followed by general exchange of opinion. "The coming Religion" was the subject of the discourse which I listened to there. As to religious opinion, each was at liberty to think quite as he chose, whatever that might be.

It was proposed to increase the common income by developing a number of industries, such as seed-growing, fruit-preserving, and job-printing, and by receiving visitors to board at the house. The spot was a lovely one for summer or winter guests. It was cooled by the ocean air but distant enough from the coast to escape its occasional harshness. In regions thus located many think that the climate obtains the best California quality. There was plentiful space on the Altrurian grounds for numerous cottages and tents in which visitors could lodge, while taking their meals at the general table. This form of half camping is much in vogue throughout the State.

There are many people in California who would have liked to live for a time in Altrurian surroundings, to study the doctrines and understand what it all meant. A residence there of some days or weeks would have been the best way to learn, and if they were not converted to the full text of socialism, they would doubtless have come forth purified by some very practical information about the expense and tedium of separate house-keeping arrangements for every two or half dozen people called a family. As an experiment in co-operative housekeeping alone Altruria was worth while, but it was also a trial of co-operative agriculture, and those who are studying how to overcome the dullness and monotony of farm life and attract people from cities to the cultivation of the soil, could find much that is suggestive in this fraternal combination. The seriously curious people, who wanted to learn to live without spending all their strength at it, would have learned how in Altruria.

I inquired of an Altrurian whether they would introduce hired servants if their boarders became numerous, and thus spoil the equal charm of the place.

He assured me that if it was necessary to employ helpers for wages, these would live as members while they stayed, and their sojourn would be made an education for them in colony life. He cited one of the previous members who was afterwards compelled to serve in a private family, and who asserted that her position was hard to endure after the equality and independence of Altruria. The Altrurian idea is evidently the solution of the painful servant problem, for it makes mistress and servant co-operators.

The journal published by the community was the chief means for diffusing the principles of the colony. It was a keenly edited weekly sheet called the *Altrurian,* and while primarily devoted to the idea of public ownership it vigorously pushed the reforms embodied in the initiative and referendum, and proportional representation. It was distinguished from some reform papers in deprecating the emphasis of class antagonisms, and in teaching that social reform will be accomplished by the united efforts of the best of all classes.

Taking a general view, the colony was strongest as an educational foundation. California is stirring for something better in the social line, and it listened attentively to those who came from Altruria, because the Altrurians had the distinction of daring to put their theories into practise. There is still some lingering prejudice against the term Socialism in California, but here were these Altrurians, hard-working, intelligent, and just like other people only better, and there was no prejudice against them. They could explain why the

United States should own its railroads and trusts and nobody took offense.

The members of the experiment from the beginning say that it exploded one famous *a priori* theory, — that men will not work under other stimulus than private property. Up till the last day that the forty who left the company after its reorganization remained, they labored faithfully, although they were to reap no reward. The difficulty was to keep some of the members from working too hard.

Both the public and philosophers seem to have made a mistake on this point. Goodwin Smith says of property: —

> Its economical foundation is that it is the only known motive power of production. Slavery has its whip; but, saving this, no general incentive to labor other than property has yet been devised.

But Mr. Smith omits to notice that public property is property, and an incentive. If a man will get a better private income, or better conditions of life, by working to increase public property, why will not public property be a better incentive to labor than private property?

The colony at length came to an honorable end, the debts contracted in the beginning proving too much of a burden. It did much for Socialism in this State, more indeed than for colony co-operation. It was a center from which clear light and good work emanated, expressing that rational and genial socialism which attracts all and offends none. It trained its less experienced members, too. Some of them went there supposing it would only be necessary to have a colony to escape from industrial hardships. They came to have smaller hope in colonies and greater hope in national and municipal ownership. Now all those who belonged that are able to do so, are working actively for the inauguration of municipal and national socialism.

On the whole, it was a healthy experiment, which was thoroughly respected, and those who found colonies hereafter will gain much by studying its history and listening to the judgment of those who were in it.

Helicon Hall

With the proceeds from *The Jungle* in hand, Upton Sinclair bankrolled the utopian colony of Helicon Hall near Englewood, New Jersey. His comments about the short-lived (six months) community and its visitors is a pleasant remembrance of things past by the long-time Socialist and novelist. The community was burned-out — like Brook Farm — but Sinclair managed to write *The Industrial Republic* during his stay there.

21. Upton Sinclair's Account

Three winters spent upon an isolated farm had taken all the romance out of the back-to-nature life for a young author. The roads were either deep with mud or cut with the tracks of sleighs, so that the only place to walk was up and down in a field, along the lee side of a fence. Also, four summers had taken the romance out of agriculture as an avocation for a literary man. The cows broke into the pear orchard and stuffed themselves and died; the farmhands who were brought from the city got drunk and sold the farm produce for their own benefit. "Away from nature!" became the slogan.

The young writer, who had been close to starving for the past five

Upton Sinclair, *The Autobiography of Upton Sinclair* (New York, 1962), pp. 127–35, © 1962 by Upton Sinclair. Reprinted by permission of Harcourt Brace Jovanovich, Inc., and Bertha Klausner International Literary Agency, Inc.

or six years, now had thirty thousand dollars, in hand or on the way, and it was burning holes in all his pockets. He had never heard of such a thing as investing money, and would have considered it an immoral thing to contemplate. He wanted to spend his money for the uplifting of mankind, and it was characteristic of him that even in the matter of getting a home he tried to combine it with the solving of a social problem, and with setting an example to his fellowmen.

As a socialist Thyrsis of course believed in co-operation, and regarded the home as the most ancient relic of individualism. Every person had, or sought to have, his own home, and there lived his own little selfish life, wasteful, extravagant, and reactionary. It did not occur to Thyrsis that not every home might be as unhappy as his own; if anyone had suggested the idea to him, he would have said that no one should be happy in a backward way of life, and he would have tried to make them unhappy by his arguments.

His plan was to establish a co-operative home, to demonstrate its practicability and the wider opportunities it would bring. There was nothing revolutionary about this idea; it was being practiced in many parts of America—only people were doing it without realizing what they were doing. Up in the Adirondacks were clubs where people owned the land in common and built individual cabins, or rented them from the club, and had a common kitchen and dining room; they ran their affairs, as all clubs are run, on a basis of equality and democracy. Only the members didn't use these radical phrases and made no stir in the newspapers.

Thyrsis, for his part, had to make a stir in the papers, else how could he find anybody to go into a club with him? He knew but few persons, and only two or three of these were ready for the experiment. How could others be found? It might have been done by personal inquiry, but that would have been a slow process; when Thyrsis wanted anything, he wanted it at once. Being a modern, up-to-date American, he shared the idea that the way to get something was to advertise. So he wrote an article for the *Independent* (June 4, 1906), outlining his plan for a "home colony" and asking to hear from all persons who were interested. Soon afterward he rented a hall, and announced in the newspapers that a series of discussion and organization meetings would be held.

Many persons came; some of them serious, some of them cranks, some of them both. The process of sorting them out was a difficult one, and was not accomplished without heart-burning. There is no standard test for cranks, and there were some with whom Thyrsis could have got along well enough but who were not acceptable to the rest of the group. There were some who quietly withdrew — having perhaps decided that Thyrsis was a crank.

Anyhow, the new organization came into being. A company was formed, stock issued, and the world was invited to invest. In this, as in other reform schemes, Thyrsis found that it was possible to raise about one tenth of the money, and necessary to put up the rest out of one's own pocket. A search was begun for a suitable building; and real-estate agents came swarming, and broken-down hotels were inspected and found unsuitable. Finally there came better tidings; some members of the committee had stumbled upon a place with the poetical name of Helicon Hall.

It stood on the heights behind the Palisades, overlooking Englewood, New Jersey, just above the Fort Lee ferry from New York. It had been a boys' school, and there was a beautiful building planned by an aesthetic-minded pedagogue who hoped that boys could be civilized by living in dignified surroundings and by wearing dress suits every evening for dinner. There were two or three acres of land, and the price was $36,000, all but ten thousand on mortgage. Thyrsis, of course, knew nothing about real estate, what it was worth, or how one bought it; but the sellers were willing to teach him, and in a day or two the deal was made.

So, from November 1, 1906, to March 7, 1907 (at three o'clock in the morning, to be precise), the young dreamer of Utopia lived according to his dreams. Not exactly, of course, for nothing ever turns out as one plans. There were troubles, as in all human affairs. There was a time when the co-operative mothers of the Helicon Home Colony charged that the head of the children's department had permitted the toothbrushes to get mixed up; there was a time when the manager in charge of supplies forgot the lemons, and it was necessary for Thyrsis to drive to town and get some in a hurry. But in what home can a writer escape such problems?

The most obvious success was with the children. There were fourteen in the colony, and the care they received proved not merely the economics of co-operation but also its morals; our children lived a social life and learned to respect the rights of others, which does not always happen in an individual home. There was a good-sized theater in the building, and this became the children's separate world. They did most of their own work and enjoyed it; they had their meals in a dining room of their own, with chairs and tables that fitted them, food that agreed with them and was served at proper hours. Now and then they assembled in a children's parliament and discussed their problems, deciding what was right and what wrong for them. There was a story of a three-year-old popping up with "All in favor say aye!"

There was one full-time employee in this children's department, the rest of the time being contributed by the various mothers at an agreed rate of compensation. Many persons had laughed at the idea that mothers could co-operate in the care of children, but as a matter of fact our mothers did it without serious trouble. There were different ideas; we had some believers in "libertarian" education, but when it came to the actual working out of theories from day to day, we found that everyone wanted the children to have no more freedom than was consistent with the happiness and peace of others.

I recall only one parent who was permanently dissatisfied. This was a completely respectable and antisocialistic lady from Tennessee, the wife of a surgeon, who was sure that her darlings had to have hot bread every day. So she exercised her right to take them to an individual home. She also took her husband, and the husband, in departing, tried to take our dining room maid as his mistress, but without success. This, needless to say, occasioned sarcastic remarks among our colonists as to socialist versus capitalist "free love."

It was generally taken for granted among the newspapermen of New York that the purpose for which I had started this colony was to have plenty of mistresses handy. They wrote us up on that basis — not in plain words, for that would have been libel — but by innuendo easily understood. So it was with our socialist colony as with the old-time New England colonies — there were Indians hiding in the bushes, seeking to pierce us with sharp arrows of wit. Reporters came in disguise, and went off and wrote false reports; others came as guests, and went off and ridiculed us because we had beans for lunch.

I do not know of any assemblage of forty adult persons where a higher standard of sexual morals prevailed than at Helicon Hall. Our colonists were for the most part young literary couples who had one or two children and did not know how to fit them into the literary life; in short, they were persons with the same problem as myself. Professor W. P. Montague, of Columbia, had two boys, and his wife was studying to be a doctor of medicine. Maybe, as the old-fashioned moralists argued, she ought to have stayed at home and taken care of her children; but the fact was that she wouldn't, and found it better to leave the children in care of her fellow colonists than with an ignorant servant.

But it was hard on Montague when persons came as guests, attended our Saturday-night dances, and went off and described him dancing with the dining-room girl. It happened that this was a perfectly respectable girl from Ireland who had been a servant at our farm for a year or two; she was quiet and friendly and liked by everybody. Since none of the colony workers were treated as social inferiors, Minnie danced with everybody else and had a good time; but it didn't look so harmless in the New York gutter press, and when Montague went to Barnard to lecture the young ladies on philosophy, he was conscious of stern watchfulness on the part of the lady dean of that exclusive institution. Minnie, now many times a grandmother, lives in Berkeley, California, and writes to me now and then.

Montague came to us innocent of social theories and even of knowledge. But presently he found himself backed up against our four-sided fireplace, assailed by ferocious bands of socialists, anarchists, syndicalists, and single taxers. We could not discover that we made any dent in his armor; but presently came rumors that in the Faculty Club of Columbia, where he ate his lunch, he was being denounced as a "red" and finding himself backed up against the wall by ferocious bands of Republicans, Democrats, and Goo-goos (members of the Good Government League). Of course the palest pink in Helicon Hall would have seemed flaming red in Columbia.

There were Professor William Noyes, of Teacher's College, and his wife, Anna, who afterward conducted a private school. There were Edwin Björkman, critic, and translator of Strindberg, and his wife, Frances Maule, a suffrage worker. There were Alice MacGowan and Grace MacGowan Cooke, novelists. There was Michael Williams, a young writer, who became editor of the *Commonweal*, the Catholic weekly. I count a total of a dozen colonists who were, or afterward became, well-known writers.

There came to tend our furnaces and do odd jobs two run-away students from Yale named Sinclair Lewis and Allan Updegraff; we educated them a lot better than Yale would have done you may be sure. "Hal" and "Up" both wrote novels, but Up was better known as a poet. Hal became the most successful novelist of his time. When he came to Helicon Hall, he was very young, eager, bursting with energy and hope. He later married my secretary at the colony, Edith Summers, a golden-haired and shrewdly observant young person whose gentle voice and unassuming ways gave us no idea of her talent. She eventually became Mrs. Edith Summers Kelly, author of the novel *Weeds;* and after the tumult and shouting have died, this is one of the books that students will be told to read as they are now told to read *Evangeline* and *Hermonn and Dorothea.* I corresponded with Hal Lewis to the end of his life, but I saw him only once in his later years — sad ones, ruined by alcohol.

We had a rule among our busy workers that nobody came to any other person's room except by invitation; so everyone had all the privacy he wanted. When your work was done, and you felt like conversation, there was always someone by the four-sided fireplace or in the billiard room. In the evenings there were visitors, interesting persons from many parts of the world. John Dewey came occasionally, as the guest of Montague. Dewey was perhaps the best-known professor at Columbia in my time, and he exercised tremendous influence upon American education, though his ideas have often been misunderstood to the point of caricature. Personally, he was a most kind and gracious gentleman. Another visitor was William James, who was perhaps the greatest of American psychologists and certainly the ablest of that time. He was open-minded and eager in the investigation of psychic phenomena, and I remember vividly sitting with him at a table watching an old lady with a ouija board. I had never seen this object before, but the old lady held it for a good and trusted friend. She held a pencil or pen in her hand and went into a sort of trance, while some force moved her hand over the board from letter to letter. In Dewey's presence her hand moved and spelled out the sentence "Providence child has been carried to bed." We took this sentence to our faithful member named Randall, who owned a small business in Providence, Rhode Island, and had a wife and child there. He went to the telephone immediately and was told that the child was ill with pneumonia.

Another guest I remember was John Coryell, an anarchist, who earned his living in the strangest way — he was Bertha M. Clay, author of the sentimental romances that all servant maids then read, and may still read. Sadakichi Hartmann, the art critic came and was one of the few who were not welcome; he sent a post-card in advance, "Sadakichi Hartmann will arrive at six P.M." and there he was, on time, but unfortunately drunk, and his companion, Jo Davidson, the sculptor, was not able to control him. When the time came for departure, he didn't want to depart but insisted on sleeping on the cushioned seats in front of our fireplace. We had to turn him out in the snow, and the next day he wrote a letter to the papers about us, and there was quite a furor.

During these months at the colony I wrote *The Industrial Republic,* a prophecy of socialism in America. I have never reprinted this book because of the embarrassing fact that I had prophesied Hearst as a radical president of the United States. He really looked like a radical then, and I was too naïve to imagine the depths of his cynicism and depravity. When in the effort to become governor of New York he made a deal with Tom Murphy, the boss of Tammany, whom he had previously cartooned in prison stripes, I wanted to tear up my book. Incidentally, I had prophesied socialism in America in the year 1913; instead we had two world wars and the Russian Revolution — and I fear that more world wars and more revolutions stand between us and a truly democratic and free society. The world is even worse than I was able to realize; but I still cling to my faith in the methods of democracy.

The Helicon Home Colony came to an end abruptly, at three o'clock on a Sunday morning. The first warning I received of its doom was a sound as of enormous hammers smashing in the doors of the building. I was told afterward that it was superheated air in plastered walls, blowing out sections of the walls. I smelled smoke and leaped out of bed.

My sleeping room was in a tower, and I had to go down a ladder to my study below; there was a door, leading to a balcony, which ran all the way around the inside of a court, three stories above the ground. I opened the door, and a mass of black smoke hit me—it seemed really solid, with heavy black flakes of soot. I shouted fire, and ran out on the balcony and up to the front, where there was a studio made over into sleeping quarters for eight or ten of our colony workers. I ran through this place, shouting to awaken the sleepers, but got no response; apparently everybody had got out—without stopping to warn me! The next day, I learned that one man had been left behind—a stranger who had been working for us as a carpenter; he had been drinking the night before and paid for it with his life.

When I came back from the studio to the balcony, the flames were sweeping over it in a furious blast. If I live to be a hundred, I shall never forget that sensation; it was like a demon hand sweeping over me—it took all the hair from one side of my head and a part of my nightshirt. I escaped by crouching against the wall, stooping low, and running fast. Fortunately the stairs were not yet in flames, so I got down into the central court, which was full of broken glass and burning brands, not very kind to my bare feet. I ran to the children's quarters and made sure they were all out; then I ran outside, and tried to stop the fall of two ladies who had to jump from windows of the second story. Harder to stop the fall of human bodies than I would have imagined!

We stood in the snow and watched our beautiful utopia flame and roar, until it crashed in and died away to a dull glow. Then we went into the homes of our fashionable neighbors, who hadn't known quite what to make of us in our success but were kind to us in our failure. They fitted us out with their old clothes—for hardly anyone had saved a stitch. I had the soles of my feet cleaned out by a surgeon, and was driven to New York to stay with my friends, the Wilshires, for a couple of days. An odd sensation, to realize that you do not own even a comb or a toothbrush—only half a nightshirt! Some manuscripts were in the hands of publishers, so I was more fortunate than others of my friends.

Two or three days later I was driven back to Englewood to attend, on crutches, the sessions of the coroner's jury. So I learned what the outside world had been thinking about our little utopia. They not only thought it a "free-love nest," but the village horse doctor on the jury thought we had set fire to it ourselves, to get the insurance. Also, and worse yet, they thought we had arranged our affairs in such a way that we could beat the local tradesmen out of the money we owed them. It was a matter for suspicion that we had got ropes, to serve as fire escapes, shortly before the fire; they blamed us for this, and at the same time they blamed us because we had made insufficient preparations – although they had made no objection to the same conditions existing in a boys' school for many years. In short, we did not please them in any way, and everything they said or insinuated went on to the front pages of the yellow newspapers of the country.

Every dollar of the debts of the Helicon Home Colony was paid as soon as my feet got well, which was in a week or two. Likewise all those persons who were left destitute were aided. I bought myself new clothes and looked around to decide what to do next. If I had had the cash on hand, I would have started the rebuilding of Helicon Hall at once; but we had long negotiations with insurance companies before us, and in the meantime I wanted to write another novel. I took my family to Point Pleasant, New Jersey, rented a little cottage, and went back to the single-family mode of life. It was like leaving modern civilization and returning to the dark ages. I felt that way about it for a long time, and made efforts at another colony in spite of a constantly increasing load of handicaps.

Army of Industry

Gerald Geraldson's account of his Army of Industry association (1914 - 18) is a candid look at a socialist effort to organize the unemployed. In a community for those who had been "crowded off the Property Band Wagon," Geraldson was able to put into practice some of the idealism that Edward Bellamy's Nationalism had fired in him as a young man. The Geraldson farm was transformed into an open community intent on aiding the propertyless.

22. Socialist Community

Up to 1914 we had a big, live Socialist Local at Auburn, California, a typical local very much like many others all over the U.S. at that time. We were constantly proselyting and constantly "doing politics." We bought and distributed much literature; voted on the incessant stream of referendums always coming along and dug up much money for various of the activities carried on by the "movement" at that time.

Out of all this activity and discussion a new idea gradually became dominant in the minds of several of us and finally came to be discussed more than any other one topic. It was that: "If the goal of all this effort is a co-operative civilization, presumably restricted in

Ernest Wooster, *Communities Past and Present* (Newllano, 1924), pp. 133-36.

some way as to the holding of property by individuals, the way to reach such civilization must lie in starting here and now and building it." . . . The upshot of it all was that finally a number of the most active, energetic members of the local closed up their affairs and went to the Llano Colony, while others joined hands in establishing a smaller "colony" on a fine fruit farm in the Sierra foothills near Auburn to give the new idea a tryout. . . .

When we started out there were quite a number of rank-and-file Socialists among us, several members of the I.W.W., and a number of persons of various other view points—about forty in all. We did not incorporate, but threw several families and several lots of property of one sort or another together tentatively, for the use of all so far as possible, for a year, agreeing to carry the enterprise on as a unit for that time and to be guided as to our future course by what we learned. And we learned a lot.

As was to be expected, when we got down to business, there turned out to be about as many different ideas as to how we were to do things as there were people in the group. Also, there was a great diversity of opinion as to how to do almost every item of the work we had in hand and as to who should do the various kinds of work we had to do in carrying on the orchard or "farm." Also, it soon developed that quite a large percentage had come with us, not for any ideal or with any sincere desire to serve, but merely to get an easy living and anything else that they could.

We reasoned from the first that the easiest people to reach and the people most in need of the relief to be offered by a co-operative activity, were those persons who had been crowded off the Property Band Wagon, who were "broke," and so we made admission to our "union" free, depending on the labor power of the members, after they were "on the job" to keep their wants supplied and the bills paid. Those of us who were in line to contribute property of any kind to the scheme presumably felt that we could add that little to our labor power in our desire to serve the common good, without any special compensation. It was all pretty vague at first, but we kept the door open anyway to the propertyless person who sought our haven, and of course, acquired a fine bunch of "getters" who wasted, stole, and destroyed faster than the others could produce, to the end that we went behind several hundred dollars a month for all of that first year. We had a good crop of fruit which sold at fair prices, but we had borrowed so much for running expenses that we came out at the end of the year poorer than we went in.

Of course, we had the typical radicals' ideas as to democracy: that each one should have a "say" about everything concerning the group and its activities, and so on. We elected a "supervisor" of the group and various heads of departments. We met often and "discussed" much, even as to how any money we had on hand should be disbursed. I recall one sharp debate as to whether we should buy clothes for the children or whiskey for the "men." We appointed committees and sent them to make purchases and did everything else about after the approved fashion. It often took us until nine or ten o'clock in the morning to argue out the details of the day's work. During the winter there was much pruning of fruit trees to do, which is urgent, skilled work. Often a bonfire was built and more talking done than pruning, to the end that we got very much behind though having three times as many men on the job as a Japanese tenant would have had. No elected supervisor of the pruning could do more than coax or scold.

At first we established a rule that each man should have five dollars Saturday night to "go to town on." As that was before the "dry" regime this sum always enabled several of them to get very drunk, made a very noticeable hole in our funds, and, of course, had a very demoralizing effect in other ways, often leading to disgraceful brawls that were witnessed by women and children, as well as to other ills. Later we reduced this "town" money to two dollars a week, but it was then used to buy alcohol and made about as much trouble as ever. To make up the shortage, fruit, chickens, and hogs were several times taken to town and sold to get money for liquor. One man took a horse and wagon for the same purpose. . . . We had valuable horses, too large for speed, ridden and driven beyond all reason; in some cases to their very definite injury, and vehicles of all kinds driven and battered to the limit.

. . . We had "Sociologists" who also managed to avoid work of any kind, but were always on hand at meal time. One fellow in particular, of this type, captured the entire milk supply on one occasion and hid it away so that he could have peaches and cream while the rest of us, except the children, were not even having milk. He was highly indignant when the milk was restored to the children and denounced the procedure as "tyranny."

We always extended the "glad hand" to strangers and lent a sympathetic ear to tales of woe, to the end that we were imposed on in endless ways by persons who came there out of curiosity or to "take a rest." . . .

Those of us who have survived have learned more about human nature than we ever thought existed. We see humans now just as lovable animals with a good deal of hair and primal instinct left and a very thin veneer of "civilization," "idealism," "altruism," attached. Even those who have had "the best opportunities" turn out to be utterly "human" when this very thin covering is penetrated. And communal activity soon penetrates the covering. We can't pose or bluff very long, and "get away with it" in the communal group. So some more "very valuable" acquisitions left us to our fate.

Here, as elsewhere, Economic Determism determines. Grocery bills, interest, taxes, and the like, shape policies and dictate methods. While these will not exist in the New Civilization, they will continue around its edges until the whole world is reorganized—that is, we shall have surpluses to sell and various things to buy. Our people were hearty eaters, wore out many shoes and much clothing, and were wasteful and expensive otherwise. Some devoted workers for the Common Good took employment on the outside and turned what they earned into the common fund, and still we went behind.

When the end of the first year came around we had a lot of problems to think out as best we could. Were we going to continue? If so, how were we going to organize? What was going to be our policy on various questions? . . . We had been gradually curbing the liquor supply by withholding money, were again denounced as tyrants and lost a family or two of wastrels, also some single men, but we had gained some valuable recruits. As far as we could reason it out we regarded our enterprise as one composed of people who did not OWN anything individually. We had found that whenever questions of ownership arose the harmony was destroyed. . . . We who had property wanted it to be held in some way so as to benefit humanity in general, not any certain group of persons. . . .

So we decided to continue, most of us. And we decided to continue to offer free admission to persons who would meet certain reasonable requirements, for we desired, and it seemed logical, to offer relief to persons who really needed it, not to persons who had more or less money and so, did not need it. Those of us at the "hub" decided that, as those already in had made no "investment," except in a very few cases, and had been admitted free, they were in no position to question or pass on the admission of others.

We maintained the group at the hub almost intact and they agreed that it was the logical thing to do in the light of our experience. Later we withdrew all consideration of money matters, of buying, selling, and so on, from the members, finding that these, like divided ownership, were "Property Activity," and all led to divided economic interests and to a divided household. We were seeking solidarity.

So a little group of us in California, working at and thinking of nothing else for nearly ten years now, have been able to uncover economic truths of the greatest importance, just as definitely as if our numbers had been vastly greater. We did not deal with selected people; with such as could pay a given fee, or persons of culture and refinement; but with just plain, every-day humans, particularly "losers" in the property game. Through fortuitous circumstances we were early led to either banish or lock up OWNERSHIP, which fact opened wide the door to economic understanding.

Llano Cooperative Colony

The Llano Cooperative Colony was founded by Job Harriman as an economic supplement to the Socialist political movement. Harriman was active in the Bellamy Nationalist movement of the nineties, the Socialist Labor Party candidate for governor of California in 1898, and vice-presidential candidate on the Debs Socialist Party ticket of 1900.

In the belief that political action ignored the economic potential of cooperative action, Harriman formed the Llano Cooperative Colony in 1914. From 1914 to 1918 some 900 socialists and union members labored with considerable success to make the arid Antelope Valley of Southern California into a garden.

In 1918 the community moved to Leesville, Louisiana, and set up New Llano. The second community was marred by lawsuits and disputes resulting in an internal rebellion in 1935 that marked the effective end of the society.

The following statement was written by Harriman in 1924 — a year prior to his death.

23. Letter of Job Harriman — Founder

In 1900 or about that time, I became convinced that the Socialist

---

Cited in Ernest Wooster, *Communities Past and Present* (Newllano, 1924), pp. 118–20.

party as a political organization was not functioning as it should. It seemed to me that the organization should be essentially a propaganda movement with political activities in such places only as there were no labor political activities, and that we should never put a ticket in the field in opposition to a labor ticket, regardless of the platform of the labor party. The reason for this attitude was the same as the reason I felt in regard to what our attitude should be toward the labor organizations. It seemed to me that the economic organization of the working class determined the political policy of the entire class just as the economic power of our capitalist class determined the political policy of that class.

It seemed to me, and I advocated it, that we should not permit any one to join the Socialist party unless he first became a member of some trade union. . . and that our propaganda in the trade-union movement should be conducted on personal lines and not in the unions during hours of business; that our members should state their position frankly and openly in regard to strikes and labor troubles, and, if the decision of the movement were against them, that it was our duty to support the strike the same as we would have supported it had we favored it, and that it should be incumbent on our members to do whatever strike or picket duty might be assigned to them, and in every way to act to their best ability to the end that the strike might be a success, suffering the loss of position or imprisonment or whatever befell those in the struggle.

. . . I held this position and frequently argued it with those prominent in the Socialist Party, but with no avail until the metal workers' strike arose in 1910 on the Pacific Coast. During that strike the Los Angeles Socialist local was induced to move to the Labor Temple and to lend every support to the union men on strike. Out of the combination there arose a joint political movement. The Socialist Party organized branches all over the city and county of Los Angeles, with a strong central committee. The Labor Unions organized a Union Labor Political Club to which they sent delegates from practically all the unions. From the Union Labor Political Club delegates were sent to the County Central Committee of the Socialist Party. This was contrary to the constitution of the Socialist Party, but there was no other way of which we knew by which the unions could be represented in the county committee, and for this reason the Constitution was violated.

A joint campaign was conducted on the enthusiasm that was aroused by reason of the strike and by reason of the arrest of the McNamaras, whom the labor movement in Los Angeles thought innocent. This created great enthusiasm, and the Socialist and Labor ticket would have been elected by a large majority had the McNamaras not pleaded guilty five days before election.

Some time after this campaign, the Socialists who were more or less opposed to the combination raised the constitutional objection with the National Committee. . . . It resulted in a complete separation of the two movements and the collapse of the Socialist Party in Los Angeles.

I was so impressed with the fact that the movement must have an economic foundation that I turned my attention to the study of means by which we could lay some such foundation, even tho it be a small one as well as an experimental one. After two or three years, I decided to try to establish a co-operative colony. This was undertaken in Los Angeles County, California, at the mouth of the Big Rock Creek, about 45 miles from Los Angeles, due north, or about 90 miles by road.

To accomplish this purpose, I proposed to organize a joint stock company in which each member should purchase two thousand shares, paying for 1000 in cash or property, and paying for the other 1000 shares by labor. The reason for this was to give each an equal voting power. . . . We provided that each member of the colony who was engaged in work for the colony, either at the colony or at some other place, should receive $4 a day. It was understood that those working in the colony should equally receive only as much as was necessary to feed and clothe them and one dollar a day as payment on their stock until their other thousand shares should be paid for, and the balance was to accumulate as credit until the net returns from the colony should be sufficient to pay them.

This would lay an economic foundation, as it seemed, of equal ownership and pay. We established at the first a social system which was free alike to all, with no charges for amusement, whether it was dancing, moving pictures, or what not. The reason for this position was that high-class entertainments could be furnished if no charges were made, whereas if charges were made, many would demand things to which they had been accustomed, and thus prevent the social uplift which we imagined would follow in the trail of refined entertainments.

These three elements, then—equal ownership, equal wage, and equal social opportunities—were the fundamental principles of the colony. . . . With these points in view I gathered eight men besides myself.

.   .   .   .   .

Having been a Socialist for 23 years and a believer in the theory of economic determinism, and in Marx' philosophy of surplus value as determined by the social labor power necessary to produce products, and the belief in materialistic conception of life, I assumed that if a co-operative colony could be established in which an environment were created that would afford each individual an equal and social advantage, that they would, in a comparatively short time, react harmoniously to this environment and the extreme selfishness and greed as it appears in the capitalist and in men of conflicting interests would be done away. It was my theory that this would be especially true if we could establish a school that would grow into a colony institution, finally engulfing all of the members of the colony in mingled educational and industrial pursuits. I was confident that the scientific knowledge would increase the efficiency in the industrial field sufficiently to allure all into the school, and that the mental development, along with the economic advantage, would work out such a degree of harmony as is necessary to the permanency of community life.

I also thot that the social relations as stated above were vital, and that every uplifting social means within our reach should be adopted as the refining influence necessary to the intellectual, cultural, and economic condition of the colony. The purpose of all this was to show that a community could live together in harmony, could produce its own living, direct all of its members, maintain a higher standard of living than is usually maintained—and all with far less labor.

I thought that if this could be done then we could use this community as an example by which other communities could be built. I realized, in a way, that the economic condition was vital, and, while I thot it was the determining factor, I still felt that a study of the mind in the most scientific way was likewise necessary, although I at that time hinged practically everything on the materialistic theory and the theory of economic determinism.

The purpose, in addition to the establishing of other colonies, was to build an institution or a colony that would have vision and a value beyond the mere welfare of the individuals in the colony, and would become a matter of large social interest, teaching the possibilities of community life.

Subsistence Farming

Utopian aspirations for the unified life did not decline with the demise of socialism as a vibrant political and moral force. As the evils of the industrial revolution became entrenched and as towns became cities, there was a slow movement toward a redefinition of community in relation to urban life. The Southern Agrarians, in an aesthetic and reactionary cry, called for a conservative return to a simpler set of values and way of life.

Ralph Borsodi's *Flight From the City* (1933) marks the beginning of the modern utopian age, since Borsodi's lament is that of the trapped urban dweller seeking some sense of physical community with the land. He sought economic independence and self-sufficiency by returning to the country in much the same way young city people move into California communes today. Borsodi's approach was a modest one, as he utilized machinery in order to eliminate drudgery yet tried to reintroduce domestic crafts (weaving, canning) wherever they seemed practical. He did help found a community in Dayton and provided a rationale and philosophy that became public philosophy in the thirties and an accepted creed in the sixties.

24. Flight from the City

In 1920 the Borsodi family—my wife, my two small sons, and myself—lived in a *rented* home. We *bought* our food and clothing and furnishings from retail stores. We were *dependent* entirely upon my income from a none too certain white-collar job.

We lived in New York City—the metropolis of the country. We had the opportunity to enjoy the incredible variety of foodstuffs which pour into that great city from every corner of the continent; to live in the most luxurious apartments built to house men and women in this country; to use the speedy subways, the smart restaurants, the great office buildings, the libraries, theaters, public schools—all the thousand and one conveniences which make New York one of the most fantastic creations in the history of man. Yet in the truest sense, we could not enjoy any of them.

How could we enjoy them when we were financially insecure and never knew when we might be without a job; when we lacked the zest of living which comes from real health and suffered all the minor and sometimes major ailments which come from too much excitement, too much artificial food, too much sedentary work, and too much of the smoke and noise and dust of the city; when we had to work just as hard to get to the places in which we tried to entertain ourselves as we had to get to the places in which we worked; when our lives were barren of real beauty—the beauty which comes only from contact with nature and from the growth of the soil, from flowers and fruits, from gardens and trees, from birds and animals?

We couldn't. Even though we were able for years and years, like so many others, to forget the fact—to ignore it amid the host of distractions which make up city life.

And then in 1920, the year of the great housing shortage, the house in which we were living was sold over our heads. New York in 1920 was no place for a houseless family. Rents, owing to the shortage of building which dated back to the World War, were outrageously high. Evictions were epidemic—to enable rapacious landlords to secure higher rents from new tenants—and most of the renters in the city seemed to be in the courts trying to secure the

Ralph Borsodi, *Flight from the City* (New York, 1933), pp. 1–9.

protection of the Emergency Rent Laws. We had the choice of looking for an equally endurable home in the city, of reading endless numbers of classified advertisements, of visiting countless real estate agents, of walking weary miles and climbing endless flights of steps, in an effort to rent another home, or of flight from the city. And while we were trying to prepare ourselves for the struggle with this typical city problem, we were overcome with longing for the country—for the security, the health, the leisure, the beauty we felt it must be possible to achieve there. Thus we came to make the experiment in living which we had often discussed but which we had postponed time and again because it involved so radical a change in our manner of life.

Instead, therefore, of starting the irritating task of house and apartment hunting, we wrote to real estate dealers within commuting distance of the city. We asked them for a house which could be readily remodeled; a location near the railroad station because we had no automobile; five to ten acres of land with fruit trees, garden space, pasturage, a woodlot, and if possible a brook; a location where electricity was available, and last but not least, a low purchase price. Even if the place we could afford only barely complied with these specifications, we felt confident that we could achieve economic freedom on it and a degree of comfort we never enjoyed in the city. All the other essentials of the good life, not even excepting schooling for our two sons, we decided we could produce for ourselves if we were unable to buy in a neighborhood which already possessed them.

We finally bought a place located about an hour and three-quarters from the city. It included a small frame house, one and a half stories high, containing not a single modern improvement—there was no plumbing, no running water, no gas, no electricity, no steam heat. There were an old barn, and a chicken-house which was on the verge of collapse, and a little over seven acres of land. There was a little fruit in the orchard—some apples, cherries, and plums, but of the apples at least there were plenty. . . . Yet "Sevenacres," as we called the place, was large enough for our initial experiment. Four years later we were able to select a more suitable site and begin the building of the sort of home we really wanted.

We began the experiment with three principal assets, courage—foolhardiness, our city friends called it; a vision of what modern methods and modern domestic machinery might be made to do in the way of eliminating drudgery, and the fact that my wife had been born and had lived up to her twelfth year on a ranch in the West. She at least had had childhood experience of life in the country.

But we had plenty of liabilities. We had little capital and only a modest salary. We knew nothing about raising vegetables, fruit, and poultry. All these things we had to learn. While I was a handy man, I had hardly ever had occasion to use a hammer and saw (a man working in an office rarely does), and yet if our experiment was to succeed it required that I should make myself a master of all trades. We cut ourselves off from the city comforts to which we had become so accustomed, without the countryman's material and spiritual compensations for them.

We went to the country with nothing but our city furniture. We began by adding to this wholly unsuitable equipment for pioneering, an electric range. This was the first purchase in the long list of domestic machines with which we proposed to test our theory that it was possible to be more comfortable in the country than in the city, with security, independence, and freedom to do the work to which we aspired thrown in for good measure.

Discomforts were plentiful in the beginning. The hardships of those early years are now fading into a romantic haze, but they were real enough at the time. A family starting with our handicaps had to expect them. But almost from the beginning there were compensations for the discomforts.

Before the end of the first year, the year of the depression of 1921 when millions were tramping the streets of our cities looking for work, we began to enjoy the feeling of plenty which the city-dweller never experiences. We cut our hay; gathered our fruit; made gallons and gallons of cider. We had a cow, and produced our own milk and butter, but finally gave her up. By furnishing us twenty quarts of milk a day she threatened to put us in the dairy business. So we changed to a pair of blooded Swiss goats. We equipped a poultry-yard, and had eggs, chickens, and fat roast capons. We ended the year with plenty not only for our own needs but for a generous hospitality to our friends—some of whom were out of work—a hospitality which, unlike city hospitality, did not involve purchasing everything we served our guests.

To these things which we produced in our first year, we have since added ducks, guineas, and turkeys; bees for honey; pigeons for appearance; and dogs for company. We have in the past twelve years built three houses and a barn from stones picked up on our place; we weave suitings, blankets, carpets, and draperies; we make some of our own clothing; we do all of our own laundry work; we grind flour, corn meal, and breakfast cereals; we have our own workshops, including a printing plant; and we have a swimming-pool, tennis-court, and even a billiard-room.

In certain important respects our experiment was very different from the ordinary back-to-the-land adventure. We quickly abandoned all efforts to raise anything to sell. After the first year, during which we raised some poultry for the market, this became an inviolable principle. We produced only for our own consumption. If we found it difficult to consume or give away any surplus, we cut down our production of that particular thing and devoted the time to producing something else which we were then buying. We used machinery wherever we could, and tried to apply the most approved scientific methods to small-scale production. We acted on the theory that there was always some way of doing what we wanted to do, if we only sought long enough for the necessary information, and that efficient machinery would pay for itself in the home precisely as it pays for itself in the factory.

The part which domestic machinery has played in making our adventure in homesteading a success cannot be too strongly emphasized. Machinery enabled us to eliminate drudgery; it furnished us skills which we did not possess, and it reduced the costs of production both in terms of money and in terms of labor. Not only do we use machines to pump our water, to do our laundry, to run our refrigerator—we use them to produce food, to produce clothing, to produce shelter.

Some of the machines we have purchased have proved unsatisfactory—something which is to be expected since so little real thought has been devoted by our factory-dominated inventors and engineers to the development of household equipment and domestic machinery. But taking the machines and appliances which we have used as a whole, it is no exaggeration to say that we started our quest of comfort with all the discomforts possible in the country, and, because of the machines, we have now achieved more comforts than the average prosperous city man enjoys.

What we have managed to accomplish is the outcome of nothing but a conscious determination to use machinery for the purpose of eliminating drudgery from the home and to produce for ourselves enough of the essentials of living to free us from the thralldom of our factory-dominated civilization.

What are the social, economic, political and philosophical implications of such a type of living? What would be the consequence of a widespread transference of production from factories to the home?

If enough families were to make their homes economically productive, cash-crop farmers specializing in one crop would have to abandon farming as a business and go back to it as a way of life. The packing-houses, mills, and canneries, not to mention the railroads, wholesalers, and retailers, which now distribute agricultural products would find their business confined to the production and distribution of exotic foodstuffs. Food is our most important industry. A war of attrition, such as we have been carrying on all alone, if extended on a large enough scale, would put the food industry out of its misery, for miserable it certainly is, all the way from the farmers who produce the raw materials to the men, women, and children who toil in the canneries, mills, and packing-towns, and in addition reduce proportionately the congestion, adulteration, unemployment, and unpleasant odors to all of which the food industry contributes liberally.

If enough families were to make their homes economically productive, the textile and clothing industries, with their low wages, seasonal unemployment, cheap and shoddy products, would shrink to the production of those fabrics and those garments which it is impractical for the average family to produce for itself.

If enough families were to make their homes economically productive, undesirable and non-essential factories of all sorts would disappear and only those which would be desirable and essential because they would be making tools and machines, electric light bulbs, iron and copper pipe, wire of all kinds, and the myriad of things which can best be made in factories, would remain to furnish employment to those benighted human beings who prefer to work in factories.

Domestic production, if enough people turned to it, would not only annihilate the undesirable and non-essential factory by depriving it of a market for its products. It would do more. It would release men and women from their present thralldom to the factory and make them masters of machines instead of servants to them; it would end the power of exploiting them which ruthless, acquisitive, and predatory men now possess; it would free them for the conquest of comfort, beauty and understanding.

Sunrise Community

The Sunrise Community was founded by Joseph Cohen in 1933 and lasted until 1936. Membership was drawn mostly from socialist and labor groups. A cooperative farm community, it ran into financial and legal difficulties and wound up in the Michigan courts. Few of its members were farmers, and a majority of them came from New York City.

The following account indicates some of the problems that urban communitarians faced on the southern Michigan frontier.

25. Community Origins

On the morning of June 27th we took over the administration of the farm. The former owners had paid off all the workers the night before, and now the responsibility was ours. We asked the employees to stay on the same basis as before, and most of the labourers were glad to do so. But there were exceptions among the supervising personnel. The chief mechanic refused to work for us under any circumstances, and some of the foremen asked for an increase in pay, so that it took most of the morning to straighten things out and set the complicated machinery of the farm working under our control.

Our hired workers, and the need to raise large amounts of money to pay them every two weeks, continued for a long time to be one of

Joseph Cohen, *The Sunrise Community* (Detroit, 1939), pp. 42–47.

our most pressing problems. On the fifth and twentieth days of each month a line stretching from the office door the whole length of a city block would move slowly forward to receive the light pay envelopes, computed at the miserly rate of 15 cents an hour. All the same, each payroll took twelve to fifteen hundred dollars to meet. In addition, we had a whole string of better-paid and steadily employed specialists; a horse man, a shepherd, two field foremen, three trac-tor-drivers, a blacksmith, an allround mechanic in charge of the power plant, grain elevator and pumps. During the second month we added an agricultural adviser; it was the old Dutchman, who had managed the farm years before. He lived ten miles away, but he came every morning and stayed as long as necessary, never showing the least fatigue, in spite of his great age. He, like the other hired people, had to be paid punctually on the days established by custom. It was not at all an easy matter for a community that had started out with borrowed money.

Our only source of income that summer was from membership fees. Great numbers of people were anxious to join us, and our representatives, Dr. M. in New York and Comrade H. W. in Phila-delphia, two devoted men who were to join us later, carried the burden of sifting out the desirable element among the many who applied for membership.

Our requirements were stringent. For example, an age limit was introduced that summer, barring all people over forty-five years of age, while large families, over-burdened with children, were not encouraged to join. Conservatives and religious people were not accepted, neither were professed Communists, whose main activity at that time consisted in disrupting labour organisations. We limited ourselves to progressive, socially-minded people from the organised labour movement, and liberal small tradesmen. In addition, every candidate for membership, and his whole family, had to undergo a physical examination, which barred many applicants. But the requests kept pouring in, and the money received from those who were accepted kept the farm going and provided the means for improving the old shanties.

Living and office accommodation, indeed, formed another of the problems we faced in the beginning. The former manager and book-keeper were staying on for a month to wind up the accounts, and they and the representative of the former owners occupied the office, while we had to shift as best we could. All the better dwellings were occupied by hired foremen and specialists, and for our members, the owners of the place, we had to use the badly dilapidated shanties. It took a great deal of work and much money to make them habitable. In the meantime, while we were waiting for the shanties, we all lived in the old dormitory which we called "The Hotel"; it had 36 small rooms, and no conveniences of any kind. We transformed the lobby, a large room equipped with a cold water tap, into a combined kitchen and dining room, where the food was prepared and served in relays to the whole group. Outside, in front of "The Hotel", there was another tap, which served the whole group for washing purposes. On the other side of "The Hotel" there was an old latrine, which had to serve the needs of men and women alike.

The first weekend after our arrival in the community coincided with the July 4th holiday, and it brought an unexpectedly large number of visitors. From as far away as Philadelphia and St. Louis, Chicago and Cleveland came interested people, and considerable numbers of sympathisers arrived from Detroit and the smaller towns of Michigan. This was partly because the newspapers of the Middle West had played up the story of a group of poor people acquiring a "million-dollar property" as they called it. The great monetary value of the place impressed the reporters, and made them treat our experiment more or less seriously. Whole pages, illustrated with photographs, were devoted to the Sunrise Community in the Sunday editions, and this made us, for the time being at least, a Mecca for all the radicals in the neighbourhood. On that first week-end we were hardly in a position to accommodate visitors, and could not even feed them properly, but nobody seemed to mind in the least; the very vastness of our lands was enough to move them to enthusiasm.

Among these 4th of July visitors there was a young physician from Detroit, Dr. Peter G. Shifrin. Dr. Shifrin had lived through the horrors of the civil war in Russia, had endured all the privations of the period of Military Communism during the first years of the revolution in that country. He was very much interested in our enterprise, and we invited him to join us and take care of the health of our members. At the time he told us that he had other plans for his future, and could not see his way clear to join an enterprise like ours. Nevertheless, a few days later, we received a letter from him, offering his services without payment for the summer. We accepted gratefully, and Dr. Shifrin joined our ranks. He immediately set up a health centre and clinic, with a few beds for minor cases, and made arrangements with a hospital in Saginaw for the treatment of any major cases that might occur.

Dr. Shifrin was a great help to us during all the years we remained in Michigan. He was an exceptionally able physician and a highly intelligent man, sincerely devoted to the interests of the community. In the fall of 1933 he took up postgraduate courses in Public Health at Michigan State College in East Lansing, 55 miles away, but he still looked after our health and we made arrangements from this time onwards to pay him a small and almost nominal sum for his services. In all, he stayed with us for two-and-a-half years, and pulled us through many difficult health situations.

But his interest in the community was a good deal more than medical, and on at least one occasion his decisive action played an important part in giving our members confidence in their own ability to overcome the difficulties they were likely to encounter in farming. One day in August, when the N.R.A. was first put into effect, we were in the middle of harvesting our grain. At that time we were still badly handicapped by the fact that none of the members had as yet any experience in handling large agricultural machinery, whether operated by teams or tractors. Yoine, the president of the community, who claimed to be an experienced farmer, actually made it a point to keep the members away from the teams and the machines. In the fall, he promised, when the harvest was in, he would take them one by one and teach them how to work with a team of heavy Belgian horses. In the meantime, we employed a number of hired men as teamsters. On that morning, the hired teamsters turned out as usual, but they sat down near the horse barn and refused to take out the teams. They did not feel like working that day, they claimed.

When the news was brought to the members of the community, who were at breakfast in the dining room, they were justly annoyed, since harvest time on a farm is not a season for whims and caprices. "Let's take the teams out ourselves!" Dr. Shifrin suggested. The men followed him with a will, He donned his overalls, harnessed the horses, and in very little time the heavy wagons were rolling behind the teams on their way to the threshing floor. Yoine was fortunately away that morning, so that he could not interfere, and this incident liberated our members from the taboo imposed by him on their handling teams and machines. From then on, most of the work was done by our members, and the number and cost of hired help were both steadily reduced. Incidentally, later that day we found that the hired teamsters expected higher pay, as a result of the introduction of the N.R.A., but did not have the courage to present a demand, so they pretended merely that they wanted to take the day off, in the hope that this would induce us to offer them more money!

Koinonia Community

The Koinonia Community (1942) of Americus, Georgia, has not only had to contend with the usual utopian problems, but has been faced with hostility from local residents. Koinonia is an interracial community founded by the late Clarence Jordan as an association of Christian fellows dedicated to peaceful methods and the agricultural life.

The following sections are from a pamphlet describing the community and a more recent newsletter.

26. History and Persecution

In November of 1942 Clarence Jordan and Martin England purchased 400 acres of eroded Georgia farm land, eight miles southwest of Americus, Ga., moved their families there and proceeded to incorporate as Koinonia Farm. In the years following nearly sixty men, women and children have come together in search of the intense fellowship and way of life which in the New Testament Greek is called the Koinonia. We have come together seeking to express to the fullest in our daily lives the Kingdom of God as Jesus revealed it. We have come from many denominations, occupations and sections of the nation. (About three fourths are native Southerners.) Some of us are whites, some Negroes. Our education ranges

The Intentional Communities (Yellow Springs, 1959, mimeographed), pp. 24–26.

from illiteracy to Ph.D. Our economic backgrounds are from middle class to poor. Some have been present from the beginning in 1942; others have come quite recently.

The farm has grown to over 1,000 acres, which until the recent attacks supported the whole community. We produce peanuts, corn, small grains, sweet potatoes, vegetables, hogs, poultry and cattle. Until it was recently destroyed we were operating also a roadside market and a mail order business for our products.

The life of the community and the recent controversial history will best be understood by examining the spiritual beliefs which brought it into being and hold us together. For we are essentially a church. We meet for worship several times a week, but we consider our total life to be religious activity, whether it be work, play, or worship. The common meal at noon each day in which the whole community shares is the principal meeting of the church.

The heart of our belief is that God is a Father and those who accept his love become children of his who accept in brotherly love all other children of the Father. This love becomes the motivation and guide for the whole life of the community. It expresses itself at several basic points:

1. Because we share this deep spiritual faith and this love for one another, we accept complete liability for the economic needs of one another. No one says that anything is his own, but all is held in common. The farm is one unit. All property is owned by the community, which is a legal corporation. This principle of common ownership characterizes any human family where real love exists. We see the Koinonia as the family of the Father which is open to all who accept this way of love. Each member gives according to his ability and receives according to his need.

2. As children of a God of Love, we believe that this love is the most powerful force in the universe and therefore no other weapons should be used in its stead in one's relationships with his fellow beings. Even enemies are to be loved, prayed for, and sought with good will. Retaliation, revenge, or violence in any form Koinonians will not use. Though we have been attacked with guns, dynamite, fire, and boycott, we have returned no violence.

3. Since love is the only requirement for those who would be children of the Father, the Koinonia asks nothing more of those who would join it. Since God has no favorite children, we have no favorite brothers. Therefore, old distinctions of race, caste or nation are given no consideration.

It is the practice of this way of life without regard to racial lines which has brought about the present crisis at Koinonia. Throughout our history there have been periods of greater or lesser tension with the surrounding community. We have tried to keep the lines of fellowship open. We have been conscious of the needs of the area and made efforts to meet them as we are able. We practiced the best methods of scientific farming and shared our knowledge with our neighbors. Koinonia pioneered in poultry layers and through our initiative the county has become one of the chief egg producing centers of the state. We have tried to do our business locally whenever possible, though sometimes savings could be had through wholesale channels.

However, with the Supreme Court's desegregation decision and the subsequent return of Ku Kluxism in the South, the tension began to rise until the situation has now become critical. The pressure began with an economic boycott, increased its intensity with legal harassment and finally exploded in violence.

In March 1956 one of the members of Koinonia, an alumnus of the University of Georgia, agreed to sign an application for two Negroes, whom he considered to be sincere, for entrance to Georgia Business College (white). He was disqualified for technical reasons, but the press gave front page coverage. The very same day threatening anonymous phone calls began to come in and egg customers began to refuse to buy our eggs. It has subsequently been necessary to sell all but 800 of a flock of 4,000 layers as a result. This boycott spread from one area to another until it is now virtually complete. Supplies of gasoline, fertilizer, butane gas for heating and cooking, and mechanical service for vehicles were refused us. Local firms will not buy our peanuts or gin our cotton. The bank with which we have had a perfect rating for 14 years cut off all credit. Insurance has been cancelled again and again, and each time was rewritten on another company, but now no company can be found anywhere in the world to cover our property.

Koinonia sponsored an interracial children's camp in 1955 and spent several thousand dollars in preparation for the 1956 season. A few days before the opening date, the county Board of Commissioners brought an injunction on grounds of "health and sanitation" prohibiting its opening and the camp had to be moved to another state. Legal proceedings stretched out over the summer until after the camp's closing date.

Violence first occurred in June, 1956, and has increased in intensity. In June a .44-calibre pistol was fired into our roadside market. July 23 a charge of dynamite wrecked this market; damage estimated at $3,000. Signs advertising the market were repeatedly torn down and finally destroyed. November 27 a newly acquired refrigerated meat case was destroyed by buckshot.

Typical of attempts to drive Koinonia out of Georgia are the following incidents:

February: Two cars fired shotgun blasts into the main cluster of residences, sprinkling with shot children playing on the volleyball court. One shot, presumed by the sheriff to be a .22 rifle bullet, entered a window and narrowly missed a child. Mid-February saw a rash of cross burnings before homes of Negroes friendly to Koinonia and an intensive campaign of rumors and threats to intimidate them. Buckshot was fired into the home of an elderly Negro couple who live on Koinonia property and work for wages. High-powered rifle shots were fired into the residential cluster, one shot narrowly missing the Jordans' daughter.

Our insurance problem is being met through a plan whereby friends are asked to sign a promissory note for $50.00. The response has been wonderful. Concern for us has also been expressed by groups of friends throughout the country who call themselves Friends of Koinonia. Their purpose is to aid Koinonia in any way possible.

We continue to feel that we need somehow to address ourselves to helping the people around us overcome the fear and bitterness which are searing their hearts. We are asking God to free us from all ill-will and self-righteousness that we might be channels through which His redemptive love might flow.

.   .   .   .   .

For a long time we have been concerned that our children played with guns, pistols, soldiers, and other toys of war while we are a community devoted to Christ's principles of love and nonviolence. What effect does it have on a child when he swaggers around with a two-gun holster, shooting everything and everybody dead? Is this something he will normally outgrow, or is it part of the psychological conditioning which ultimately glorifies war? Should we "tolerate" this in our children, or forbid it, even though they might hanker all the more for the "forbidden fruit"?

We decided to call a meeting of all our school children and explain our dilemma to them. An exciting, and sometimes heated discussion ensued in which even the first graders shared their feelings. Finally they unanimously agreed that somehow guns and Jesus don't go together and that perhaps they'd better just get rid of their guns. Later we had a special "peace" service, at the close of which each child brought all his war paraphernalia and placed it in a garbage can to be burned. Then the community presented each one with a new toy or game, and we all joined in singing the spiritual, "Ain't Gonna Study War No Mo'."

At the present there are no Negroes living at Koinonia. However, our hearts and our doors will always remain open to all people of all nations. We say this not in defiance of those who oppose us, but in humble submission to Him who has called us and to whose purposes we have dedicated ourselves. We do continue to have fellowship with those who are not afraid to have associations with us.

Intentional Communities

The term "intentional community" has come to replace the older "communist" or "socialist" label and reflects (as did the earlier change) an attempt to broaden the community movement by neutralizing the generic term. However, recently the term "commune" has been put into use again in a linguistic move back to an original American form.

Since the mid-sixties there has been a dramatic resurgence of interest in communitarianism. A revolt against the Vietnam War and a technocratic society coupled with a widespread use of drugs combined to produce dropouts who sought an alternative culture. There is no single coherent philosophy — as with Owenism or Fourierism — but an amalgam of attitudes and ideas that are pacific and egalitarian. California and New Mexico have the largest concentration of communes, although Boston and Washington, D.C., both support sizable "free communities" composed of radical theater groups, underground newspapers, and political "communes."

Because the modern art forms are music and film, little literature has been produced by the most recent communists. This is partly due also to the lack of clearly defined community goals, since the present movement exalts both personal identification and awareness along with the corporate life. Such potential contradictions between a "do your own thing" philosophy and a community effort have not been examined. So far the impact of the new communes has been miniscule; nevertheless the existence of an alternative culture based on self-reliance and the simple life may suggest other methods to less hip groups.

The following statements represent a range of recent attitudes, from Christian to Aquarian.

27. Fellowship of Intentional Communities

For purposes of membership in the Fellowship of Intentional Communities an intentional community shall be a group of people associated together for the purpose of working out a whole way of life in general harmony with the concepts and principles set forth as characterizing the spirit and purposes of the communities at present members of the Fellowship. While the practice of community should be visible in all fields, we feel it must in this age emphasize particularly the economic on the one hand and the spiritual on the other and it must include both production and use.

Size — the minimum size should be three families or five adults.

Organization — The group should be sufficiently organized to be a recognizable social entity acting with responsibility and effectiveness.

Location — The group should share land and housing or be otherwise close enough together geographically to be in continuous active fellowship and be able to work out effectively the total way of life to which they are dedicated.

BASIC CONCEPTS

Most of the following concepts are in the background thinking and feeling that has gone into the establishment of each of the communities belonging to the Fellowship.

1. Community means mutuality and sharing in a whole way of life, in all its values and all its responsibilities.
2. The essence of community is spiritual, that is, the feeling of

The Intentional Communities (Yellow Springs, 1959), pp. 2–3.

mutuality, the practice of mutual respect, love and understanding. No physical forms or practices will create community,
but forms, methods and practices will grow out of the spirit.

3. The ultimate worth of personality; the importance of respectful,
understanding, and kindly relationships; the superiority of living, emotional, cultural and religious values; the ultimate community of all mankind: these concepts enter into the purposes
and goals of intentional community.

4. Participation in community is essential to maturing individual
personality on the one hand, and the practice of community is
essential to maturing human society on the other hand. Intentional community facilitates both.

5. Intentional community is an effort to create a social order
which may in time become more universally accepted and so
help to create the inclusive human community where the normal thing is to practice mutual concern, respect and love and to
share cooperatively and democratically in the responsibility,
work and use of the values of life.

6. Small groups of people intentionally dedicated to a mutual
concern to share in the responsibility and work of creating the
values of a whole way of life, to share the daily round and the
special emergencies of life, to endeavor that each and all may
enjoy life's values fully, and to work these purposes out in
mutual love and respect are engaged in intentional community.

7. Community in concept, practice and experience is a matter of
growth. All groups begin immaturely. Maturity increases
through devotion, experience and open-minded humility.

PRINCIPLES

The following principles are agreed to be essential, and most of
them are the current practice in communities now members of F.I.C.

1. Democratic methods. Either Rochdale principles or Friends
methods of business are used to carry on business and effect
community action.

2. Nonviolent methods. Dependence upon violence in conflict or
to gain community ends is outside the purpose and practice of
intentional community.

3. Some effective sharing of economic possessions and spiritual resources. It is felt that the critical test of community in our times is in the field of economics where current mores rests so large a share of interest, and in the spiritual field where ideologies are born and purposes, relationships and goals are sustained.
4. Freedom to evolve a way of life. Hence unwillingness to tie community to a static goal, e.g., a home for a specific class of people, or promotion of a specific conviction. Hence also the effort to work out from an inward spirit and conviction unbound by words and definitions.
5. Concern for a balance between the worth of the person and the place of the social whole.
6. Desire for fellowship with other persons and groups without regard to race, class or religious extraction.

28. Communities and Communes

The New Age which the radical movement is working to create is one which the idea of community is of vital importance. In this column I am not going to write about why it is good but how to deal with some of the problems which the worker for and participant in will find as a community is created?

What is a Community?

A community is any group of people who are living together in fairly close physical proximity, i.e. a village or a rural commune.

What is a Commune?

A commune is a group of people who are sharing a major part if not their entire lives together and are living in a single building or a group of buildings developed for the purpose, i.e., a kibbutz or a Hutterite settlement.

Roger Wilks, "Communities and Communes," *The Green Revolution,* June, 1969.

The problems which are faced by any community or commune can be divided into two main groups — those of a physical nature and those of a psychological nature. From time to time in any growing community the dominance of problems will vary. As a simple example it is not serious to suffer from a shortage of water for washing and drinking for a day or two but for two or three weeks there develop not only health problems but also interpersonal ones arising from the stress created by the water shortage. In this case it is of little use to deal with the interpersonal problems before dealing with the water shortage.

In the other direction you will often find that marriages break up when the couple join a community or more especially when it is a commune. The surface reason may be that one partner cannot stand the sharing of the bathroom; to build an additional bathroom is not likely to solve this problem. In all likelihood the real cause is that the marriage which might have been very good outside the commune developed to meet certain demands which have gone and there is little or nothing remaining for the couple to share except past memories.

In building a commune we must always be aware of both types of problems and lay our plans accordingly. In selecting the site for the commune we must consider the number of people who can be housed adequately and fed without imposing an overwhelming strain on the physical plant. In developing our commune we must also consider how we will deal with the various problems of interpersonal relationships.

There is a third area from which a threat to the growth of a community both physical and spiritually comes and that is the larger community outside our microcosm. It is certain that the larger community will have many doubts and reservation about us. We either implicitly or explicitly represent a threat to their way of life. This threat is the same as the one I mentioned earlier about marriages being broken up after the couple have entered a community.

Having written of problems, how can we overcome some of them?

In the case of the outside community one good rule is make sure that you are familiar with the local health and building code. Copies of these can be bought from the county in which the community exists. These codes will tell you what are the minimum requirements for a building to house a given number of people in terms of space, toilet facilities and about six million other details. In most areas it is possible to exceed their demands for space and other facilities, provided that you show you are working towards meeting their requirements. The speed at which you are making progress can often be very elastic.

With regard to your neighbours there is one very pleasant fact about country life and that is the willingness of many straight people to help you. To meet these people, go to country auctions and talk to them, offer your help with the local volunteer fire department. You will certainly get cracks about long hair and hippies but if you offer warmth you will get it back. If a farmer offers advice on planting and gives you seed at least try hard to plant the seed and cultivate the land. When the crop comes in ask him and his wife around to try some or go over and give him some of the crop. By doing this you will help make a friend for your community and you will have another source of useful information.

29. Community for the New Age

So you want to be able to speak with animals? So do I! Perhaps I cannot tell your fortune or cast your horoscope, but I can tell you what your deepest longings are; even the longings that you have never shared with any other person.

You long to have "impossible" freedoms. You want to be so free that you could just flap your arms and fly through the air; even to travel through space and visit other worlds! You wish you could be completely open and honest with everyone, having no need to be ashamed, also about your body; you would be fully known and understood and be able to comprehend all other living things, so that nothing would need to be hidden at all.

You want tremendous adventures and you want them to be mean-

Art Rosenblum, "Community for the New Age" (published by the author). Art Rosenblum is the Director of the Aquarian Research Foundation, Philadelphia.

ingful and important, but at the same time you long for a beautiful security; the certainty that you will never have to grow old and die.

Am I writing in an unknown language? All quite mad? Or is it rather that we have grown up in a dying society which never dares to speak of the things that humans really want—like the Spaniards of old who risked their lives to travel to a "new world," openly admitting that they hoped to find the fountain of youth?

Well, let's get down to earth, then. We hear talk of revolution by people who don't always know what they mean by it, but we already see changes and a new morality that encourages us to be free with our bodies. But the old order tries to make us think that we are "sick" if we would be completely free to be seen just as we really are, and be free to express a warm affection for other people in a physical as well as a spiritual way. It is as if only war and killing could be the true mark of manhood. Haven't we had enough of that swindle? Isn't it time to find out what being human really means?

Good news was called "gospel" in Greek and the good news was that a new age was coming for all the world; not some old tale about burning in hell if you didn't do what the priests (and the state) demanded. Perhaps some of you can put a few things together and sense that the longings we have in common and the "more abundant life" that the good news speaks about are really the same thing. The real revolution that we want is the coming of the new age of love to this whole planet and to all the universe as well.

If we only look at the social unrest among students, workers, and poor people, as well as the growing disgust with the "Vietnamese experiment," and at the beginnings of disaffection within the military, we can see all the signs of a bloody and chaotic revolution or possibly civil war in the offing. Perhaps we go around in a fog because we can't fit these things together into a unified picture. But when seen as part of a new age coming, birth pangs of a new creation, it does seem to make a lot of sense. Let's get at the facts to help change come quickly through joy instead of slowly through all possible violence and suffering.

For some of us, at least, this must now become a full time commitment. We must get together in a much closer way, find new answers, and do new things. I feel that a very close and intimate form of community life would be the best environment in which to find new answers. Such a life arises when the spirit of love leads people so closely together that they are willing to share many things for a common purpose.

Deep insights come to us intuitively when we are open to receive them, test them, and act upon them. Such togetherness and loving activity would describe the kind of community that is needed. To start such a community we would have to begin by learning to listen to one another with our hearts. We would also have to listen to the spirit which works through our intuition. We would then want to live together so that a great deal of time could be given to an intimate sharing of emotional and personal problems, and learning new ways to solve them. We have to become free enough to listen to and express the most unusual concerns.

I have visited many different communities and have lived in some for sixteen years altogether. Some of these groups have found effective ways of solving emotional hang-ups, and these ways should be learned.

Social changes must happen so fast that there is no time for violence! I have come to believe that the violence which threatens us today is not caused by the rapidity of change but by resistance to it. We have failed to understand the meaning of our most basic longings, and failed to realize how fully these longings are shared by other people. If that resistance could be broken down and all our longings known and understood, then great changes could come in beautiful ways.

Many ways to do this can already be suggested, and in a sensitive, listening communal life, better ones would surely pop up.

One suggestion that the community could undertake would be the setting up of block radio stations operating by carrier current and therefore requiring no FCC license. Many colleges have such stations, and experiments have shown them to be capable of covering more than a city block.

Whenever possible, income for the community should be provided by the kind of work which would fit the concerns we have; selling movement literature, or special types of education such as helping parents to understand their radical teenagers, might also be a source of income. The commune must also provide room for visitors and new members; must be ready to expand and help new groups start,

but it could not become a crash-pad for people who are not serious
about the purpose of the group.

In the next few years, or even sooner, this country will likely
experience a great upheaval. If it is not a revolution of joy, it could
be a bloody civil war. War can come easily, but joyful transformation requires great daring and togetherness. We need people who are
ready to drop everything else and begin the new life.

30. Family Living: A Radical Solution

The radical left movement has long protested the existing economy, and has assumed the responsibility of continually seeking a
better solution to contemporary conditions. A basic change in
life-style is the most obvious method of attacking the bond to the
established quagmire. Communal living has proved to be a successful alternative to the single family unit, and has provided valuable
resources to the movement.

Living in single family units, the establishment has us right where
they want us. We are urged to be economically independent from
each other, encouraged to be possessive of our material assets in
every way, encouraged to believe that we cannot trust our brothers
to care about us and that we should therefore not care about them.
The media leads us to believe that only consuming more products
will relieve us of the constant pressures we feel in this oppressive
society by showing us that happy, fulfilled people use their product.
If we are frustrated and unhappy, the blame must lie within ourselves and we must not reveal ourselves too closely to others. We
must mistrust others' interests in our personal lives as a direct threat
to our self-reliance. We are, therefore, forced to compete with each
other almost constantly—for the most beautiful body, the nicest
home, the best stereo tape recorder, the latest gadgets on the market,
even for the most "well-adjusted" children.

We can refuse to be pigeon-holed by society into subhuman existence through communal living. We can begin by making physical
existence less expensive. Group living begins by sharing the largest

"Family Living—A Radical Solution," *The Green Revolution,* June, 1969.

expense of all, the house. If ten people share a house payment of $200/month, each person only pays $20/month as rent. As each person saves money he could well use for something else, he also denies the establishment that amount of support. This holds true for all the other things shared within a commune; the appliances, furniture, the radios and TVs, the utilities.

Because communal living costs less, each individual is set free from the economic necessity of working at a dull, frustrating job because he can't afford to take one that pays less. He is also free to work part time if he wants more time for other activities, or is free not to work at all if there is the need. Housecleaning, yard-work, and general maintenance are much less time consuming and burdensome when the responsibilities are shared. The aspect of substantially increased free time is doubly important to the movement because of all the things that need to be done, but are now being done by just a few people. Communal living would give those already deeply involved some time to themselves and would give others time to become more involved. Related to this is the aspect of group living as an educational tool. One is exposed to a much more diverse store of knowledge than in a nuclear family situation. This is mentally stimulating and enjoyable, and especially helpful to the movement when ideas of radical change are shared.

In a communal setup there is a great emphasis on human relationships. This pushes the value of consumer products even lower than it already is in many of our minds. Human relationships can also become much more satisfying when those in the group are honest about their feelings towards themselves and towards each other. There is new perspective put on relationships when members of a group share their observations and feelings about those relationships. The deeper and more important human relationships become to an individual, the less he cares or even thinks about being a consumer and loyally supporting the market. This puts us exactly where the establishment does not want us. And a very important place for us to be.

31. The Post-Competitive, Comparative Game of a Free City

Most of the modern community literature emphasizes the "counterculture" theory that pits the "people" and their life style against the exploitative establishment. The establishment of free cities within urban centers assumes a community that is forced to act because of oppression and is intentional only because their real human needs have been ignored by the powers that be.

Our state of awareness demands that we uplift our efforts from competitive game playing in the underground to the comparative roles *of free families* in *free cities.*

We must pool our resources and interact our energies to provide the freedom for our individual activities.

In each city of the world there is a loose competitive underground composed of groups whose aims overlap, conflict, and generally enervate the desired goal of autonomy. By now we all have guns, know how to use them, know our enemy, and are ready to defend. We know that we ain't gonna take no more shit. So it's about time we carried ourselves a little heavier and got down to the business of creating free cities within the urban environments of the western world.

Free Cities are composed of Free Families (e.g., in San Francisco: Diggers, Black Panthers, Provos, Mission Rebels and various revolutionist gangs and communes) who establish and maintain services that provide a base of freedom for autonomous groups to carry out their programs without having to hassle for food, printing facilities, transportation, mechanics, money, housing, working space, clothes, machinery, trucks, etc.

At this point in our revolution it is demanded that the families, communes, black organizations and gangs of every city in America co-ordinate and develop Free Cities where everything that is necessary can be obtained for free by those involved in the various activities of the individual clans.

"The Post-Competitive, Comparative Game of a Free City," *The Realist,* 81 (August, 1968), 15–17.

Every brother should have what he needs to do his thing.

Free City

An outline . . . a beginning
Each service should be performed by a tight
gang of brothers whose commitment should enable
them to handle an overload of work with ability
and enthusiasm. 'Tripsters' soon get bored, hopefully
before they cause an economic strain.

Free City Switchboard/Information Center

should coordinate all services, activities, and aid and direct assistance where it is most needed. Also provide a reference point for legal aid, housing, machinery, etc.; act as a mailing address for dislocated groups or individuals and guide random energies where they are most needed. (The work load usually prevents or should prevent the handling of messages from parents to their runaway children . . . that should be left up to the churches of the community.)

Free Food Storage and Distribution Center

should hit every available source of free food—produce markets, farmers markets, meat packing plants, farms, dairies, sheep and cattle ranches, agricultural colleges, and giant institutions (for the uneaten vats of food)—and fill up their trucks with the surplus by begging, borrowing, stealing, forming liaisons and communications with delivery drivers for the left-overs from their routes . . . best method is to work in two shifts: morning group picks up the foodstuffs and the afternoon shift delivers it to the list of Free Families and the poor peoples of the ghettoes. everyday. hard work.

This gang should help people pool their welfare food stamps and get their old ladies or a group to open a free restaurant for people on the move and those who live on the streets. Giant scores should be stored in a garage-type warehouse equipped with freezers and its whereabouts known only to the Free Food Gang. This group should also set up and provide help for canning, preserving, bread baking, and feasts and anything and everything else that has to do with food.

Free City Garage and Mechanics

to repair and maintain all vehicles used in the various services. the responsibility for the necessary tools and parts needed in their work is entirely theirs and usually available by maintaining friendly relations with junkyards, giant automotive schools, and generally scrounging around those areas where auto equipment is easily obtained. The garage should be large enough and free of tripsters who only create more work for the earnest mechanics.

Free City Bank and Treasury

this group should be responsible for raising money, making free money, paying rents, for gasoline, and any other necessary expenses of the Free City Families. They should also organize and create small rackets (cookie sales, etc.) for the poor kids of the ghettoes and aid in the repair and maintenance of the machinery required in the performance of the various services.

Free City Legal Assistance

high-style, hard-nosed, top-class lawyers who are willing to defend the rights of the Free City and its services ... no honky, liberal bleeding heart, guilt-ridden advocates of justice, but first class case-winners ... turn on the best lawyers who can set up air-tight receivership for free money and property, and beat down the police harassment and brutality of your areas.

Free City Housing and Work Space

rent or work deals with the urban gov't. to take over spaces that have been abandoned for use as carpentry shops, garages, theatres, etc., rent whole houses, but don't let them turn into crash pads. Set up hotels for new arrivals or transients by working out deals with small hotel owners for free rooms in exchange for light house-work, porter duties, etc. Big warehouses can be worked on by environmental artists and turned into giant free dance-fiesta-feast palaces.

A strong trio of serious business-oriented cats should develop this liberation of space within the cities and be able to work with the lawyers to make deals and out-maneuver urban bureaucracies and slum landlords ... one of the main targets for space are the churches who are the holders of most real-estate and they should be approached with a no-bullshit hard-line.

Free City Stores and Workshops

nothing in these stores should be throwaway items . . . space should be available for chicks to sew dresses, make pants to order, re-cut garments to fit, etc. The management should all be life-actors capable of turning bullshitters into mud. Important that these places are first class environments with no trace of salvation army/st. vinnie de paul charity rot. Everything groovy. Everything with style . . . must be first class. *It's all free because it's yours!*

Free Medical Thing

should be established in all poverty areas and run by private physicians and free from any bureaucratic support. The Free City Bank should try to cover the expenses, and pharmaceutical houses should be hit for medical supplies, etc. Important that the doctors are *brothers* and do not ask to be salaried or are not out to make careers for themselves (witness Dr. David Smith of the Hippie Free Clinic in San Francisco who is far from a brother . . . very far).

Free City Hospital

should be a house converted into bed space and preferably with a garden and used for convalescence and people whose minds have been blown or who have just been released from a state institution and who need the comfort and solace of their people rather than the cold alienated walls of an urban institution.

Free City Environmental and Design Gang

gangs of artists from universities and art institutes should be turned on and helped in attacking the dank squalor of the slums and most of the Free City Family dwellings . . . paint landscapes on the sides of tenements . . . fiberglass stairwells . . . make crazy. Tight groups of good painters, sculptors, designers who comfortably construct environments for the community. Materials and equipment can be hustled from university projects and manufacturers, etc.

Free City Schools

schools designed and run by different groups according to the con-
sciousness of their Free Families (e.g., Black Man's Free School,
Anarchist's Creative Arts School, etc.). The schools should utilize
the space liberated for them by the Free City Space Gang.

Free City News and Communication Company

providers of a daily newspaper, monthly magazine, free Gestetner
and printing of notices for other groups and any special bulletins and
propaganda for the various families of the Free City. The machinery
should be kept in top condition and supplied by any of the various
services. Paper can be scavenged at large mills and cut down to
proper working size.

Free City Events . . . Festival Planning Committees

usually involves several Families interacting to sponsor tours for the
kids . . . Balls, Happenings, Theatre, Dance, and spontaneous experiments in joy . . . Park Events usually best set up by hiring a
20-foot flat-bed truck for the rock band to use as a stage and to
transport their equipment; people should be advised by leaflets to
bring food to exchange with their neighbors; banners, props, bal-
loons, kites, etc. should be handled by a committee; an electrician
should be around to run the generator and make sure that the P.A.
systems work; hard work made easy by giving responsible people
the tough jobs.

Co-operative Farms and Campsites

the farms should be run by experienced hands and the Free Land
settled on by cottage industrial people who will send their wares into
the Free City. The farms must produce vital food for the families . . .
some free land that is no good for farming should be used as
campsites and/or cabin areas for citizens who are in need of country
leisure, as well as kids who could use a summer in the woods.

Scavenger Corps and Transport Gang

is responsible for garbage collection and the picking up and delivery
of items to the various services, as well as liberating anything they

think useful for one project or another. They are to be responsible for the truck fleet and especially aware of the economic strain if trucks are mis-used by tripsters.

Free City Tinkers and Gunsmiths, Etc.

will repair and keep things going in the houses ... experienced repair men of all sorts, electricians, and carpenters. They should maintain a warehouse or working space for their outfit.

Free City Radio, TV and Computer Stations

demand Free time on radio and TV stations; demand a Free City frequency to set up your own stations; rent computers to call the punches for the revolution or use them in any constructive way possible.

Free City Music

Free Music
Where is the place that your music comes from
do you know
What determines the rest between phrases
The Interval that grows from the cluster
of sounds around it
Hanging behind the beat
Clipping the front of it
That's the gift
The thing that blows through a body that responds to
spirit and a mind that doesn't lock itself
It's that thing
We're all made of, forget about, and then try to grab again
That thing that's all there and all free
The fretless infinite string banjo has invented new means
of music which it must buy from itself to sing

.   .   .   .   .

fat man owns the carnival and all the booths play business. he double hypes the want glands, lets *you* buy in and then displays what's available to the crowd. all of a sudden you got something to lose. he spreads the news and pays for it by telling kids they're ugly blemished smelly unimaginative and dull ... then sells them cures, says to you, "here kid, change the name, change the games, do anything you want, but don't give it away." that game's called vested interest and it can apply to anything.

fat man runs a crumby joint, but it's the only joint right?

He'll be there until we free the goodies

ı

Ma-Na-Har Cooperative Community

While *The Realist* suggests a raid on the local butcher, the older agricultural plan seems to predominate, with a heavy dosage of experimental education in the New Harmony tradition. The Ma-Na-Har Community statement of aims and goals is moderate and as of 1971, it was working.

32. Principles

Ma-Na-Har Cooperative Community is located on the land belonging to Bhoodan Center of Inquiry of Oakhurst, Inc., near Oakhurst, California, about half way between Fresno and Yosemite Valley on Highway # 41. Visitors from the north should cut across to Highway # 41 from Madera on Highway 145. Turn east at Oakhurst onto Road # 426, go 4½ miles to Bhoodan Center's mailbox and sign. Turn left onto dirt road and follow the signs. There is no public transport nearer than Fresno or Madera. We are in the Sierra Nevada foothills at 3,000 ft. elevation.

The major possibilities for employment here are largely seasonal, in logging, lumber mills, Sierra National Forest, and resorts. Population of Oakhurst is about 2,000.

There are public elementary schools. The high school is now 60 miles away by school bus. Plans are developing for a new high school at or near Oakhurst.

There are several churches and a Seventh-Day Adventist private

---

Ma-Na-Har Cooperative Community (published by the community).

grammar school. The religious affiliation of the original members of Ma-Na-Har is Society of Friends (Quakers), but our community is completely open to people of various religions or philosophies.

No illegal drugs are permitted here. Most of the members and affiliates do not smoke or use intoxicating liquors and we would like for their rights to be respected on the same basis as others expect their rights to have these things.

Purposes

1. To help one another in seeking spiritual as well as intellectual guidance and direction and to seek ways we can apply such guidance in our lives.
2. To work together toward creating an environment where we can be of mutual assistance to one another in learning to fulfill life's purposes and provide our needs, in order that we can be of worth to ourselves and others.
3. To seek out and experiment in ways to coordinate our activities that will build toward the best life for not only ourselves, but our entire society — toward the "brotherhood of man."
4. To cooperate with Bhoodan Center of Inquiry of Oakhurst in carrying out its purposes of research, experimentation, and education in the problems of living.
5. The eight principles of Bhoodan Center shall also be the principles by which this community shall be guided and shall function.

Membership

The membership will begin with the original committee for organization, who are:

Charles W. Davis   Larry Quiring

Catherine Davis   Madelle Quiring

The community will become more formally and more thoroughly organized as more people participate in it.

There are certain things we feel we have learned from the experiences of other communities. One of these is that a piece of shared land or a set of bylaws do not make a community. Community can only be built on harmonious, purposeful human relations. Therefore, we feel that people need to take sufficient time to *grow* into community until they mutually feel that they belong together. It is on this basis that we expect to welcome new members.

Decisions

The organizing committee and the members shall strive toward unanimous decisions in managing the affairs of the community.

Projects or Activities

The committee for community organization is starting with the projects already existing among the people who are cooperating and working with Bhoodan Center.

These projects are:

1. *Learning* — children and adults have taken an interest in, and are learning in the following fields of endeavors:
   a) American history
   b) Human relations
   c) Music
   d) Folk-dancing
   e) Arts and Crafts — We have experimented with production for our own use, such as leather work, pottery, weaving, etc.
   f) Harmony with Nature
   g) Religion (Search — not dogma)

2. *Cooperative Equipment Sharing*
   a) Carpenter hand tools
   b) Mechanics hand tools
   c) Chain saws
   d) V.W. Bus and Land Rover
   e) Auto repair shop
   f) Gas Welder
   g) Electric Welder
   h) 4′ × 8′ trailer
   i) 2 ton GMC truck

Individual members who wish to participate in maintaining tools or cars for use under cooperative arrangements and who are willing and capable of proper understanding of use and care may be accepted into the group which operates this pool.

3. *Purchasing and Exchange*

Those members who wish to cooperate with this committee and are willing to share the responsibility as well as the benefits are buying together in quantities for a better price and choice of quality. There are three ways we exchange (including labor):

a) Some things we sell for cash.

b) Some things we trade.

c) Some things we share with others who need them.

4. *Experimental Work in Mountain Agriculture* (Begun by Larry Quiring and Catherine Davis)

The objectives are to try to find:

a) What things can be grown on sloping mountain soil and where there is some scarcity of water.

b) The best methods to use in mountain areas.

c) Ways to produce the food, fibre, and forage to reduce the amount of cash needed to be earned on jobs, and to have better, fresher foods.

5. *Food Preparation*

Besides the production projects we also buy and trade for food at the peak season and process it by drying, freezing, and canning.

6. *Employment Pool*

Much of the employment in this area is seasonal. Jobs are accepted for members of the community that provide short or part-time work, such as: carpenter work, remodeling, maintenance work, orchard work, building fences, care of children, etc.

This allows making enough money to provide needs but also free time for pursuing creative objectives and activities.

Must People Conform?

Although we believe in freedom (with responsibility), there are some things we have to conform to within the community in order to attain our objectives and pursue our search for a better and more whole life.

1. We must be open to learn and to try out new and different ways (since change is one of our objectives).

2. There should be no yearning to be elsewhere (for the culture of the city, or home and mother).
3. There should be sufficient commitment to some accomplishment with the others in the community — so temporary inconveniences do not deter or cause one to give up.
4. One must accept, at least temporarily, the way the community is trying to do things. We cannot change with each person who comes here. There must be a very good and basic understanding of how we are trying to do things, before we are expected to accept suggestions and make changes.
5. Everyone must verbalize and share their thoughts. Community is impossible without communication.
6. Everyone must try very hard to not alienate others by what they say, do, and how they act.
7. Everyone must be concerned and responsible — must care about others as well as themselves.

Differences and Change

We feel that one of the ways in which our community is unique is in the fact that we do not wrap it up neatly, tie it with a bow, and say, "This is how we are going to do things," or, "This is what we base our community on." We do not say, "Now we are all going to be vegetarians, or all live communally, or all farm for a living, or practice Zen, and this will then constitute the basis of our community." The basis of our community is human relations. We say only that we will come together and work on our problems and help one another and experiment with different ideas. Also, no one has to be involved in all the projects going on, but may choose to work in the areas he is interested in. Not allowing for the inevitable growth and change in the human animal has been responsible for the failure of many communities.

We do not expect all to be alike, to have the same abilities, to contribute equally in the group. Everyone, however, should do his part as he can toward the total efforts. At the same time we should appreciate each according to his ability.

Communal Living

Those of us here now are not in favor of strictly communal living, with everyone living together in one residence and interacting with each other day and night and sharing everything. We share many things, but on a voluntary, not a compulsory basis. We have developed a closeness among us and are learning a great deal about human relations by experience, but, although it is necessary now with our limited facilities, we do not plan to always live so physically close nor to always eat communally.

However, we welcome to our community those who do believe in a more communal approach. A way could probably be worked out for them to live as they wish and grant us the same privilege. We believe that people must be free to use their initiative and creativity. At the same time we need to find ways that we can relate to each other though we differ. We are working on ways that people can have freedom even though they must be responsible to others with whom they are involved. In order for people to proceed on this basis there must be open and free communication at all times.

Learning

We have come to recognize that all of life is experimental, from moment to moment and day to day. We never really know how anything that we decide to do will turn out until we have tried it. We can hardly assume that we have arrived at final knowledge in anything. When we look at details of our lives or at the major projects of humanity in the world we immediately see that there is much to change, improve, learn how to do better. We, at Ma-Na-Har, are deeply conscious of the need to learn. For this reason we usually speak of ourselves as an experimental community.

In line with this, we try to avoid the use of the word education and use the word learning instead, with the concept that learning comes not only from formal institutions, but from all of life. Equally true is the fact that none of us should ever stop learning. Formal education may end with high school or college but learning should be a continuous part of our lives. In our community we have several specific areas of learning in which all ages are participating together.

About Children

There are many things of value in the kind of community we are trying to build. The community situation is a very special one for children. At Ma-Na-Har it is encouraging to see everyone take an interest in the children and help them or take time with them. In a house on a city block, without community, there are only the parents. Here our children are exposed to different points of view and they learn how to interact, relate, and get along with many different kinds of people. All ages take part in most of our learning situations.

We must recognize that children are people. They only have certain differences. They are usually not as tall of stature and may not know as many things as adults. However, their curiosity, and speed of learning are better than older persons'. They often speak great wisdom that is worth heeding. Community can only be normal and the best if it has all ages in it. Children can contribute some values, older people others. We can all receive some benefits from others, regardless of age, and we can all be responsible to contribute something to others.

Relationship with Nature

Most of the members of our community are intensely aware of the interdependence of all life (as our name implies). Some are more interested in the study, observation, or communion with nature than others.

The manure from the corral and the scraps from our table make compost to fertilize the garden. Our closeness to the changing seasons, the water in the spring, and our location in the Sierra Nevada foothills all serve to remind us daily of the chain of life.

The ecological balance is being destroyed so many places in so many ways, and conservationists are fighting such uphill battles. We believe that man is more whole if he lives so that he is able to observe and relate to his natural environment. We must not lose sight of man's relationship to all life, nor his responsibility toward it.

Though some of our members are very interested in nature or believe in relating very closely to it, this does not mean they can sit around all day and smell the flowers while the others struggle with the problems. The work of our community must be shared by all. However, we do fit the interest of the individual to the job, somewhat, in that those most interested in nature are the ones who are working on the organic garden and orchard at the present time. These people take responsibilities in other areas as well, however.

The Wider Community

We feel we have to work with one foot in the system while we are working to change it — partly because we do not really see another way, and partly because the people in society as it is are of value also. If they cannot be helped to see the need for change then the necessary changes will never come about. We, therefore, make every effort to maintain a rapport with the wider community and we cooperate with them whenever we can. All of these people have something to contribute. Even those persons most opposed to our views must count with us — though we must not let them weaken us. Therefore, we must find ways — not so much for like-minded people to get along — but ways in which people who differ can learn to understand and respect one another, and incidentally keep from killing each other.

Visitors

A limited number of visitors are welcome if they arrange ahead of time and are willing to fit into our routines. We are busy trying to learn how to build our facilities and get our community going, but we take time for a wide variety of interests and activities.

People who attend the Bhoodan Center seminars, volunteer workers helping to build Bhoodan Center, and visitors from other communities usually can make arrangements to stay with families of Ma-Na-Har Community. Arrangements to share the living expenses can be worked out, with consideration for the costs and the ability to pay. The cash costs are usually about $1.50 per day for adults, $1.00 for children 12 and under. Everyone who can is expected to take turns with living chores.

How Do We Grow and Expand?

We do not pretend to have all the answers, and lest we sound slightly Utopic, we have plenty of problems and some disagreements. However, we don't believe in separating when we differ, but in working out the problems. Our community is in need of people who are willing to work with us and we would like to have more people permanently, especially families, but we cannot house them on our property now. We are trying to find housing in Oakhurst, where those who are interested in working with us may stay until more accommodations are built.

Our funds are few and therefore we have to work out ways we can finance what we are doing together. So far we have all found ways to earn the money we need and ways to build what we have with minimum capital, by doing it ourselves. Although land prices are rising, it would be good for some people to buy acreages near us and work with us here or hold the acreage until Bhoodan Center can purchase it.

BOOK MANUFACTURE

American Utopianism was phototypeset by Allied Typesetting, Dexter, Michigan. Printing and binding was by NAPCO Graphic Arts, Inc., Milwaukee. The cover design was by Evelyn Hansen. Internal design was by F. E. Peacock Publishers, Inc., art department. The type is Times Roman.